MASKS.

MASKS.

By Jamie Shalleck

A Subsistence Press Book

The Viking Press   New York

Also by Jamie Shalleck
Tea.

DESIGNED BY SAMUEL N. ANTUPIT

Contents

NO MAN, FOR ANY CONSIDERABLE PERIOD,
CAN WEAR ONE FACE TO HIMSELF,
AND ANOTHER TO THE MULTITUDE,
WITHOUT FINALLY GETTING BEWILDERED
AS TO WHICH MAY BE THE TRUE.
—NATHANIEL HAWTHORNE, *THE SCARLET LETTER*

Introduction

Which mask are you reading through? What have you done so far today to change your face? Make-up? Eyeglasses? Contact lenses? A shave? Or have you merely assumed the intangible mask of the attentive reader?

Masks are familiar social accouterments, but very few of us recognize them as such. Perhaps we have not taken the time to look or perhaps our stereotyped notions are blinding us: the masks we recognize most easily are those primitive tribal offerings that hang useless and out of context in our museums. They seem to be pathetic, even spiritless remains of another social mode which is unrelated to our current needs and interests.

But here and now masks do prevail—masks that we all wear, whether consciously or unwittingly. With a little practice, one can recognize them easily.

Let's begin with a definition. A mask is some alteration of the face—a change of appearance for purposes of protection, make-believe, social acceptance, disguise, amusement, or religious devotion. A mask is the spirit realized— inner urges given shape and form and displayed upon the face. A mask is also a medium through which the gods can be invoked. It is an invitation to the gods to inhabit an appropriate and available form, the mask itself, in order to communicate with the human tribe. A mask can attract or repel, reassure or frighten. Masks can be utilitarian or decorative or both.

Contemporary mask-makers include companies that manufacture gas masks, women who make themselves up, surgeons who perform cosmetic surgery, and political public-relations consultants.

We wear masks every day—when we put on sunglasses, apply cosmetics, wear veils, don goggles, or peer out at the world through glass windows. Masked and masking, we proceed through life, modifying our appearance to suit the occasion or the drama.

It is interesting to speculate that our curiosity about one another—our desire to meet and understand other social creatures—has something to do with the masks we wear. In fact this curiosity may be nothing but the wish to discover the rationale for a particular mask, the extent of an individual's mask wardrobe, or the "true" face behind the recognized mask. Because our society is complex and each of us is called upon to play a variety of roles which may not always be complementary, few of us can afford to go about bare-faced. One can argue that we are never maskless; honesty can be a mask.

Masks function in a variety of ways. Generally speaking, there are three types of masks: decorative, protective, and professional.

Decorative masks are optional and arbitrary. They are selected and worn in response to fashion and social demands. The individual need not wear such masks; he chooses to do so because of the way he wants to relate to society. In other words, the decorative mask is a means of communicating with society. To some extent, it alters the relationship of the individual to the group. Essentially aesthetic in effect, the mask is worn by choice to express or repress certain states of mind, emotion, belief. Decorative masks range from beards to veils, from party costumes to lifted faces. They convey a full range of values—from honesty to hypocrisy, modesty to licentiousness.

Protective masks are created in response to specific hazards. They are largely but not entirely functional. A protective mask may be modified in design for appearance's sake; sunglasses, for instance, are functional but are selected aesthetically. A mask may originate as protection and also establish itself as the badge of a particular profession—surgical masks are a typical example. But as long as the mask is worn primarily as a safety measure, it will be classified as protective.

Professional masks are difficult to define because in most cases they began as decorative or protective gear and only with time and usage did they become trade marks. But because their primary use is now that of denoting professional status, they fall into a category of their own. The wearer acquires social status because he wears a mask—e.g., the Lone Ranger. In fact, bandits' masks first served to protect outlaws from being recognized. But as crime-detection methods improved and highwaymen became local celebrities, the mask no longer protected but rather announced the highwayman in society. The mask became a status symbol, enhancing a man's professional standing. Today professional masks of all kinds help the individual achieve certain career goals.

Decorative Masks

VEILS

FASHION ACCESSORIES

MASQUERADES

HALLOWEEN

CLOTHES AS MASKS

BEARDS

COSMETICS

PLASTIC SURGERY

Decorative Masks

The face is the most complicated surface a human being projects to the world. Functionally, it allows us to breathe and eat, therefore to live. It is empowered with the senses of sight, smell, and taste, and thus determines our perception of the world. And its form determines a large part of what we call beauty—society's perception of the individual.

The face is a medium of communication, and if one were to prevent or alter the nature of that communication, a mask must be applied. The instinct that makes children (and ostriches) run away from something they fear by hiding their faces is the simplest expression of this fact. When one prevents his face from sensing danger and relaying that danger to his consciousness, the danger does not exist for him. If the face is hidden or disguised so it can not express inner fears to others, they will not recognize cowardice. Masks, like the natural face, are the superficial expression of the self—but of the self we choose to be. Masks let us be what we want to be, see what we want to see.

Though the veil does not hide the face completely, it shades it, surrounds it, confines it. Functioning as a decorative mask, the veil puts a visible distance between the wearer and the world. Aloofness, modesty, coolness, seriousness replace involvement, emotion, responsiveness, and mirth.

In Biblical times, aloof Hebrew women wore veils as a status symbol; modest Christian women were admonished to wear veils to cover their heads in church. Self-denying women in the Near East wore veils long before Mohammed (570–632 A.D.),[1]* though the practice is usually linked to Islam by angry Western feminists. In 1909, M.E. Hume-Griffith observed in her book, *Behind the Veil in Persia and Turkish Arabia,* that

> " When Mohammed, acting under what he declared to be a revelation from Allah, introduced the use of the veil, he swept away for ever all hope of happiness for Moslem women. By means of the veil he immured them for ever in a living grave. 'Imprisoned for life' is the verdict written against each Moslem woman as she leaves childhood behind her. Before the days of Mohammed the Arabs were in the habit of burying alive yearly a certain number of new-born girls; surely the fate of these innocents was better than that of the millions of women to-day who are buried alive behind the veil. "[2]

The Koran asked only for a sense of modesty in contrast to the moral laxity that had reigned—only that women "should not make an exhibition of their beauty." But in the years of Moslem conquest, from contact with conquered subjects, the Arab character was shaped into the patterns of excess and indifference that baffle modern observers. Female modesty was enforced by law; every woman was required to wear a veil. Today, however, the woman's role, even in Arab society, is changing. Veils are no longer requisite, and only the most traditional or ill-used women will wear the mask of modesty.

---

* Numbered reference notes begin on page 157.

4.

Not so in the West, where many young women gladly wear a wedding veil. The use of wedding veils in modern-day ceremonies derives from the Eastern custom of arranged marriages, in which the bride remained unseen by her husband until the ceremony had been performed. Then, he alone could know her; she remained veiled to the rest of the world. There are also some classical precedents: in Rome, pagan brides wore yellow veils; Christian brides wore veils of white or purple.

But veils were not really common usage until the end of the eighteenth century. Until this time, the wedding veil was only a (poor) substitute for long, flowing hair, which also symbolized maidenly modesty and restraint. Thus, for Elizabeth Stuart, daughter of James I of England, the veil was unnecessary. Heyward chronicled: "At length the blushing bride comes with her hair disheveled aslant her shoulders." The first American bride to wear a veil was George Washington's adopted daughter, Nellie Curtis. It was not until 1867, when a machine for making tulle was invented, that white wedding veils became standard equipment for the bride.[3]

Mourning veils are a persisting European custom. For at least a year after the death of her husband, the pious widow wears black and covers her face with a crepe veil. The veil signifies the depth of her sorrow, but it also helps her observe the social propriety of remaining aloof from frivolity and joy in memory of and respect for the dead. Though this once-common custom has itself died out in more sophisticated communities, one can still see widows dressed in black in smaller villages.

Because it isn't easy to be frivolous when wearing a black veil, "taking the veil" is also a metaphor for entering religious orders. The expression signifies the marriage to religion, renunciation of the world, assumption of the mask of devotion and spirituality. Not incidentally, in years past, ladies of the Court who had fallen out of favor voluntarily joined or were exiled to the nunnery. They exchanged the masks of aristocratic license for those of sobriety, modesty, and devotion.

For a short period of time at the end of the nineteenth century, veils were promoted as fashion accessories, despite the objections of concerned ophthalmologists who outlined the negative effects of chenille dots on the visual field. According to Casey A. Wood, author of *The Wearing of Veils, and Its Effects on Eyesight* (1896), "The least objectionable veil is that without dots, sprays or other figures, but with large rectangular meshes made with single, compact threads."[4] But the eye doctors were vindicated by public opinion. Veils never really caught on for long. Women may play at modesty for a moment, but long-term commitment to such noncommunicativeness via the veil must seem ridiculous in a society that respects communication and involvement.

But masks need not restrain. By truly hiding the face, disguising the emotions, and removing the responsibility that comes with public recognition, other, less diaphanous masks encourage women to do as they please.

During the European Renaissance, black velvet masks were fashionable accessories. In France they were called *loups*, or wolves, because they were supposed to have frightened young children. According to the English chronicler Stowe: "Women's Maskes, Buskes, Muffs, Fanns, Perewigs and Bodkins were first devised and used in Italy by Curtezans, and from thence they came into England about the time of the Massacres in Paris."

Railing against the abuses of nature and the fashion excesses of his times, Philip Stubbs wrote in 1583:

> " When they use to ride abrod they have invisories, or visors made of velvet, wherwith they cover all their faces, having holes made in the[se] against their eyes, whereout they look. So that if a man that knew not their guise before, should chaunce to meet one of them he would think hee met a monster or a devil, for face hee can see none, but two brode holes against her eyes with glasses in them. "[5]

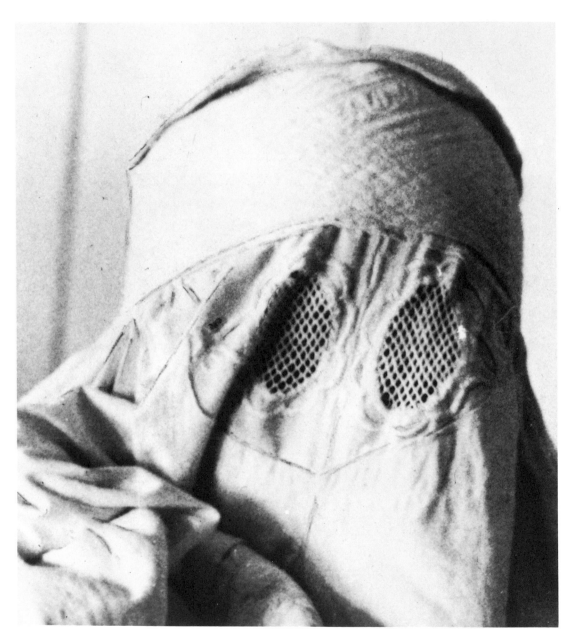

PAKISTANI WOMAN WEARING A PURDAH, OR VEIL.

By the end of the sixteenth century, masks were extremely popular among noblewomen. They were worn to the theater, when theater-going was considered risqué. They were worn in the sun by ladies who cherished pale complexions. As they came into common use, they were no longer carried in the hand or tied about the head with strings, "but held before the face by means of a slender wire and button which was placed between the teeth."[6]

Such disguises had obvious uses.

"   In a dissolute court like that of James I, the mask was an essential, and was worn upon all public occasions, even in the chase. The few ladies who dared to appear in public without this disfigurement were termed 'bare-faced.' One lady in particular, the Countess of Bedford, braved the court remarks, and, in 1613, Chamberlain wrote that she forbears painting, which makes her look somewhat strange among so many vizards, which with their frizzled powdered hair makes the ladies look all alike. Masks were small, and did not cover much of the face. Sir John Harrington, in 1606, says: 'the great ladies do go well masked, and indeed it be the only show of their modesty, to conceal their countenance.' Ben Jonson alludes to them, and Middleton, in 1611, makes various references to women's masks in 'The Roaring Girls.' Painting and patching, as well as masking, were fashionable.   "[7]

Certain primitive African tribes believe that a man in mask is possessed by spirits and thus no longer constrained to act according to human law.[8] In time, the Europeans discovered that masks allowed civilized men and women a degree of freedom that they could not experience otherwise. Soon they were wearing masks to engage in illicit or immoral activities. Prostitutes wore masks. Political intriguers arranged for masked meetings at odd hours of the night. Lovers met in mask at the opera.

Because so many people who wore masks did so to indulge in socially unacceptable behavior, all maskers risked their reputations. After Pepys bought his wife a mask, she had several unpleasant encounters with dissolute courtiers. In fact, the masks themselves came to be considered corrupting influences. Governments, anxious for order, banned them. Louis XIV's Lieutenant-General of Police, La Reynie, legislated against the wearing of masks in church.[9] He may have feared that the immorality lurking behind the mask would corrupt this bastion of social order.

*H*alloween and masquerade balls are ritual celebrations of the mask as a device permitting respite from social and moral law. The pattern of officially sanctioned reprieve from social constraints began early among civilized people conscious of social and religious order, occasionally oppressed by moral guidelines. The Roman Saturnalia was a temporary return to a Golden Age of Saturn, when license was the rule. Criminals went unpunished, social rank dissolved, serfs mimicked nobility, and the elite cavorted without dignity. A similar lack of order was permitted by the medieval Church during the Feast of Fools, when animals were ushered into Church buildings, clerics masked themselves as bishops, and priests rode piggy-back up and down the aisles of the cathedrals.

Later, in Catholic countries, the sanctioned tribute to Chaos was carnival. The Church allowed a bit of masked revelry to intrude upon its usual sobriety. Carnival was (and in some countries still is) a moment's indulgence before the penance of Lent. According to one contemporary account of carnival in eighteenth-century Italy:

> " It is a continual coming and going, a procession, an antheap of masked figures, a noise that is deafening. . . . A harlequin murmurs sweet nothings into the ear of a young woman in a domino who laughs and takes refuge among the crowds. A *mattacino,* in white with red garters and red shoes, throws

12.

egg-shells filled with rosewater at patricians' windows. When night falls lanterns twisted with flowers are hung at the doors of the houses. Within there is feasting to the sound of pipe and viol. Everyone wears a mask. Old and young, patricians and plebians, rich and poor, are all disguised. "[10]

In England and other Protestant countries, where there were no carnivals, masquerades were strictly secular affairs, held in the pleasure gardens such as Vauxall and Ranelagh. Victorian repressions, like Church morality, may have required temporary relief. Soon no one needed the excuse of carnival. The masked ball was accepted as an antidote to all forms of social repression.

In America as well as in Europe, masked balls became the rage. A newspaper, the *New York World* of December 24, 1869, prudishly described the Société des Bals d'Artistes affair:

" The Dancing commenced at 11 o'clock. At that time the floor, extending from the edge of the dress-circle to the extreme limit of the stage, presented a curious spectacle. Probably there were a hundred masked women present, among five hundred masked and unmasked men. These women were dressed in fancy costumes, nearly all selected with a view to expose as much of the person as possible. . . . There was no attempt on the part of the men to assume imposing or elegant disguises. The cheapest dominoes, and generally nothing more than a mask, afforded them all they wanted—the opportunity to carry on a bravado and promiscuous flirtation with these women. At the end of the evening the masqueraders were revealed: The panting women in the delirium of excitement; their eyes, flashing with the sudden abnormal light of physical elation, bound and leap like tigresses; they have lost the sense of prudence and safety. Some of them are unmasked, and reveal

13.

the faces of brazen and notorious she-devils, who elsewhere
are cut off by edict from this contact with the public; a few of
them are young, and would be pretty but for the lascivious
glare now lighting their faces and the smears of paint which
overlay their skins; all of them are poisonous, pitiable
creatures, suffering now with the only kind of delirium which
their lives afford, rancorous, obscene, filthy beauties, out
of the gutter of civilization, gone mad with the license of
music and the contact of men, and beset by crowds of
libidinous and unscrupulous ninnies who, anywhere else,
would be ashamed of their intimacy, or roughs to whom this
kind of a ball affords the only opportunity to exercise the
few animal faculties that are left to them.   "[11]

In the twentieth century—when world wars interrupted social
and political stability, and license was permitted under the banner of patriotism—
the masquerade was redundant, anticlimactic. Indeed, it disappeared. A soldier's
uniform was mask enough.

Postwar elation carried with it its own morality; and incipient
modernity was celebrated as brash moral and sexual freedom. The masked ball was
no longer a public necessity. It went underground, becoming a private party theme.

Though billed as the masquerade of the century, Truman
Capote's 1966 party at the Plaza Hotel in New York was surprisingly somber.
"Everyone" was there, presumably enjoying himself, but the party remained
proper, a tribute to the sobering black-and-white theme or an indication that carnival
masks are only encumbrances to people used to wearing more subtle social face
coverings.

While the masquerade has become a private celebration Halloween has
become an American institution, perpetuated by commercial costumers and by

14.

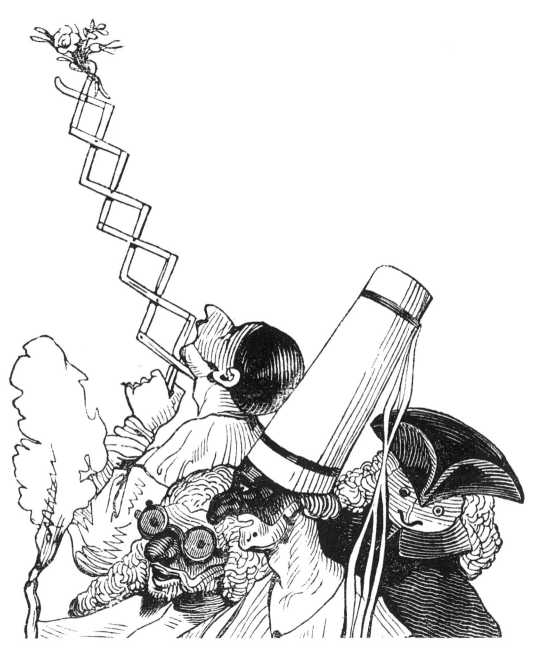

ITALIAN CARNIVAL MASKS.

children who revel in the annual opportunity to threaten usually untouchable adults with "Trick or Treat." Halloween was not always a children's game. Only in the past century or so has it been given over to the very young, perhaps the one group in our society that though repressed has failed to rebel, and so may require the release of the masquerade.

Halloween derives from pagan Scottish and Irish folk customs. On November 1, the Druids honored Samhain, Lord of the Dead. At this time, he reputedly assembled the souls of all those who had died during the year and who were taking temporary abode in the bodies of animals while expiating their sins. Samhain then released these souls to ascend to Druid heaven.

When the Romans arrived in Britain, they outlawed the human sacrifice that had been associated with these festivities. But the general outlines of the occasion held. Black cats, horses, and oxen were substituted for the human beings (criminals) that had been burned in wicker cages.

While these folk celebrations continued, the Church attempted to upstage the pagan rites by creating its own All Saints' Day, or Hallowmas, entered on the Church calendar during the eighth century, a tribute to unknown saints. November 1 was the day the spirits of the dead were sanctified. The following day, All Souls' Day, was a time of almsgiving and forgiveness, the feast of intercession for the souls of the dead.

Meanwhile, outside the Church, the folk rites grew more and more elaborate: fairies, goblins, and other pagan creatures joined the ghosts assembled by the Lord of the Dead. But these were harmless superstitions. More threatening to the Church was the association of this time of the year with witchcraft— a cult of perversity organized in opposition to the Church, with the determination to subvert Catholic ritual, reverse its litany, and praise the forces of Evil. "Halloween became the great witch night. The Prince of Darkness and his cohorts, the witches and warlocks, gathered to mock the church's festival of All Saints by unholy revels of their own."[12] In retaliation, the Church borrowed the sacrificial

16.

SUSAN BURDEN WEARS HER OWN FACE AS A MASK AT THE CAPOTE BALL IN 1966.

fires, associated with the celebration of Samhain, to burn these witches.

Because of its Catholic connections, Halloween never became an English custom. But Guy Fawkes Day occurs on November 5, commemorating the 1605 discovery of the Gunpowder Plot to assassinate James I by blowing up Parliament when he was present. During this celebration, people dance in the streets carrying effigies of "The Guy," begging pennies, and cavorting around bonfires and fireworks.

Settlers coming to America brought with them shreds of these celebrations, which gradually merged in the American Halloween. Halloween became a night of "Trick or Treating," harmless pranks, and masquerades, with costumes frequently representing the witches, black cats, skeletons, and ghosts associated with the pagan ritual. The ubiquitous jack-o'-lantern may be none other than Samhain himself, or perhaps a characterization of Guy Fawkes and his fiery plot.

Halloween, as a masked festival, rightly belongs to the young, who are honest enough to enjoy wearing a mask. They do not have to tote around the subtle masks that adults constantly wear—social roles, political poses, etc. For them the mask is a vacation from real life, a foray into make-believe.

Clothes as masks are not only for the very young, not only for Halloween. Great numbers of young people in our society understand the ways in which clothes can be used as masks to express the whim of the moment, some interest or urge, and, of course, for amusement. Clothes are costumes; costumes are masks that let us pretend to be anything we want to be.

When Charles Reich, a recent authority on the young, insists they do not wear masks, he does not allow for the many uses of masks.

"   But the costumes of the young are not masks, they are expressions of an inner, perhaps momentary state of mind. The individual is free to be inventive, playful, humorous. A boy can wear a military dress jacket, all buttons and brass, and both mock the military establishment and at the same time

> express his small-boy's love of uniforms, and parade-ground
> pomp. Likewise with a Mexican peasant's blanket-shawl, or a
> David Copperfield hat, boots of all descriptions, gangster
> suits, phantom-of-the-opera cloaks. These costumes do not hide
> the real person as a role-dress does, they show a state of
> mind and thus reveal him to us, and they add to the gaiety
> and humor of the world. "[13]

A perfect definition of a decorative mask—a mode of communication, a means of expressing feelings and emotions—humor, decoration, a game.

True, there was a time in the not-so-distant past when fashion dictated proper and improper attire. Clothes were then the mask of the initiate, like tribal markings or tattoos. Now that the tyranny of fashion has abated somewhat (thanks perhaps to the failure of the midi), clothes, indeed physical appearance in general, can be considered the mask of individual spirit, the expression of one's inner being, a picture of what one person wants to be—maybe just for the moment, a momentary truth. With this assumption, psychologists now study modes of attire. People carefully select what they will and will not wear, changing their clothes according to their moods as well as to suit the occasion.

One element of fashion that obviously functions as a mask is the beard. Grown naturally or pasted into place, it does not conceal one's identity but works more subtly, suggesting certain psychological and sexual characteristics. Because the beard is essentially a mark of physical maturity, people tend to associate it with psychological maturity as well. They think of bearded men as sophisticated, even wise, possessing the wisdom gained with age and experience.

Visually, the beard adds weight to the face—a heaviness that suggests dignity, pomp, strength, and masculinity. Frequently, a weak face can be strengthened by the addition of a beard. If nothing else, hair will cover the receding or double chin associated by amateur physiognomists with weakness or femininity.

Psychologists are at pains to demonstrate that men who wear beards are socially aloof, and that shaving the beard will make the man more responsive to the people around him. Some psychologists go so far as to suggest that shaving has created a culture that worships youth and fails to distinguish between the sexes.

In the seventeenth century, when full-blown wigs were fashionable, beards disappeared. Perhaps the atmosphere of effeminate decadence that reigned in the Courts of England and Europe and was manifested in elaborate coifs and wigs, discouraged men from wearing beards, which were blatant advertisements of masculinity.

Recently, there has been a marked resurgence of the beard. Hair has become a symbol of rebellion, a sign of honesty and forthright protest in a world of bare-faced deceit. The clean-cut American ideal was a mask that failed. It is hopelessly outmoded, a vestige of the 1950s, insufficiently convincing to disguise what was really going on. It was a pose of high morality in a world of self-seeking commercialism. For a while it worked. Americans really did believe—and wanted to believe—in God, Country, and Apple Pie; but we have become more sophisticated, and the old mask no longer fits. Furthermore, it was never designed as a battle mask for a complexly immoral war, and, when used as such in Vietnam, it fell to pieces.

In the long run the mask is a medium of truth—the truth of what the wearer is or desires or wants to be. Few Americans could convince themselves for long that all was truth and honesty and goodness when the fruits of industrial labors were polluting the environment and the costly, bloody efforts of our armies were having no visible political results. Young people, uncomfortable with hypocrisy, needed a mask that would announce their disillusionment. Beards and unkempt appearance in general became the mask of protest and despair. But even this is nothing new: hermits and religious zealots have long known the uses of dishevelment as a symbol of their moral separation from society.

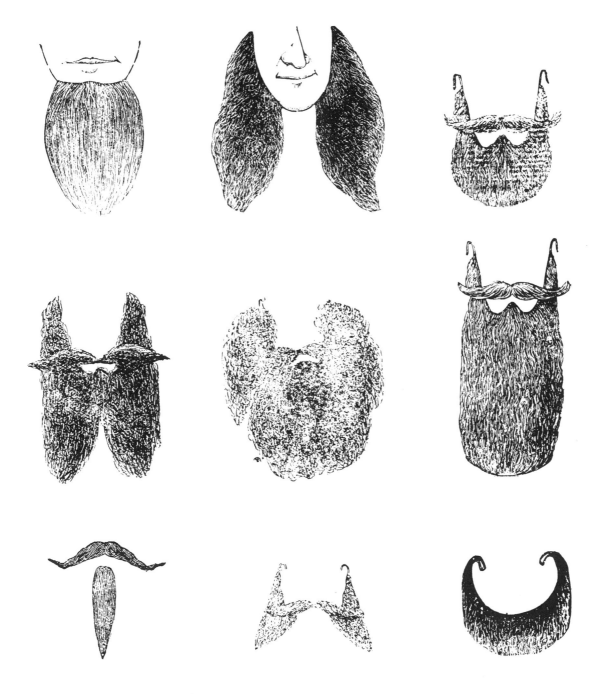

Turning away from industrial America, young people turned toward Nature; and seeking a positive, organic way of life, they boasted the mask of the primitive man—unshorn, unshaven, unrestrained.

Cosmetics also advertise the individual—what he wants to be. Perfumes, salves, incense, and paints were used by primitive man to make his body more attractive to the deities. Paint and perfume drew the gods' attention to sacrificial victims; body paint was used by tribesmen seeking divine aid in battle, in the hunt, and on other ceremonial occasions. Among civilized peoples, cosmetics were first used to avoid offending the gods with human body odor. Instead, incense and perfume would waft toward the heavens, cajoling the gods, inviting them to listen to human prayers. As society grew more sophisticated, cosmetics acquired secular uses. Just as they made humans more attractive to gods, so they made humans more attractive to one another. Civilization implies etiquette, which means not offending one another. Cosmetics, perfumes, and incense in particular, disguised the animal odors and made human company more pleasant. It can be argued, therefore, that cosmetics are a civilizing influence.

The ancient Egyptians were firmly committed to the use of cosmetics. The Ebers Papyrus (ca. 1500 B.C.) contains recipes for hair dyes and restoratives, aromatics, and skin treatments.[14] Though there may be some question as to whether or not such concoctions as cow's blood and prayer will really restore color to gray hair, there is little doubt of the lasting efficacy of the Egyptian formula for cosmetic embalming: the brains and viscera were removed from the corpse and replaced by myrrh and frankincense, the body wrapped in gum-saturated linen, masking the appearance and the odors of death.

Egyptians also beautified themselves in life. According to Dr. Henry Goodman, Cleopatra "made use of cosmetics in the limited sense of applying green paint underneath her eyes; black pigment to the eyelids, lashes and eyebrows; and henna colors to the fingernails and to the palms."[15]

22.

The ancient Hebrews learned cosmetology from the Egyptians, and later the Greeks practiced these beautifying arts. The Greek communities, with their concern for public life, their appreciation of the human body, and their cultivation of earthly beauty, helped secularize cosmetics. Perfumes and paints became so popular with Greek citizens that Solon had to pass a law prohibiting men from buying aromatics so there would be an adequate supply for the ladies and the priests. Hippocrates was not above suggesting recipes for a pimple lotion, freckle remover, and hair restorative.

Ovid noted the preoccupation with beautification:

" The women dye their hair with German herbs, and the artificial color is better than the natural. They come and go decorated with false hair which they purchase to cover their own age-worn crowning glory. Nor do they hesitate to use rouge. They wish to appear like as can be to the younger women who parade about the temple of Hercules. "

He recommended subtlety: "Hide the tricks of your beautifying arts. It is offensive to see the evidences of powder too thickly applied, or of ointments spread to excess. Keep in seclusion while in the midst of your beautifying activities, for though such actions may serve well, it is not pleasing to watch their application."

The Four Books of Cato, quoted by the medical authority Galen, comprised a pharmacopoeia of cosmetics—hair restoratives, antiperspirants, skin lighteners and conditioners. Galen himself is credited with the invention of cold cream.

At the beginning of the Middle Ages, cosmetology was a branch of medicine. Greek and Latin medical treatises, containing among other things references to the cosmetic arts, were compiled, condensed, and translated, and in this boiled-down form preserved for the Middle Ages by monks and clerics in the West, Arab scholars in the East. As the Middle Ages progressed, these compendiums were re-edited, recompiled, retranslated, and inevitably plagiarized

23.

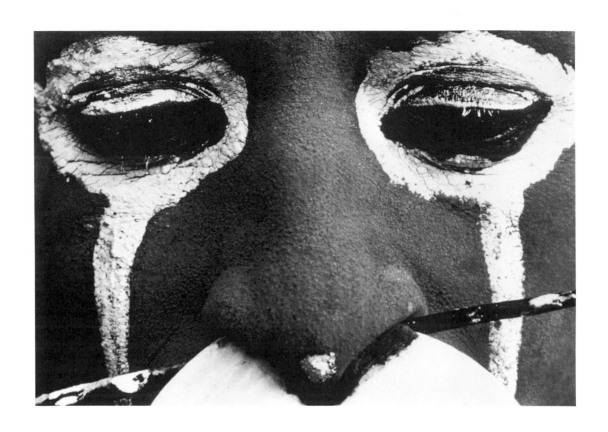

CEREMONIAL FACE PAINT, NEW GUINEA.

COSMETIC FACE PAINT, NEW YORK.

101791

by medical "authorities." Needless to say, by the time the classic texts reached the practicing physician, the medicine was thoroughly diluted. Yet some essence of Hippocratic and Galenic thought survived in the medieval medical tracts.

These medical tracts, written in Latin and the vernacular, almost always included a regimen of health, or recommendations on cleanliness. Those written in the vernacular were available to the wealthy laymen as well as to the physicians and priests, and so were more likely to include cosmetic recipes. In *Medicine in Medieval England*, C.H. Talbot explains:

> " There is scarcely a book on medicine from medieval times which does not include some recipes for colouring the hair, keeping it bright and curly, preventing baldness, and making the eyelashes and eyebrows grow long. Indeed, in a society that evidently placed great emphasis on beauty, the cosmetic arts were intensely cultivated: all kinds of facial cosmetics for preserving and softening the skin, for ridding oneself of pimples and other blemishes, for giving a rosy complexion, for making the eyes clear and bright, and much else are listed even in such scholastically toned works as those of Gilbertus Anglicus, Arnold of Villanova, John Gaddesden, John Arderne and many others. "[16]

In Chaucer's day, ladies of pretension heightened their brows by shaving back the hair at the forehead and mercilessly plucking their eyebrows; in addition, they painted both cheeks and lips with rouge. Chaucer himself seemed to prefer beauty untainted by cosmetics. His personification of beauty in *The Romaunt of the Rose* was a cheerful, unaffected, young woman of light complexion, with straight yellow hair, who needed no artificial adornments.

> " Fetys she was, and smal to see;
> No wyndred browis hadde she,
> Ne popped hir, for it neded nought

To wyndre hir, or to peynte hir ought. ”[17]

Chaucer longed for simple beauty in vain. The women were too busy painting their faces to heed the romantic longings of a poet.

During the Renaissance, painting of all kinds was celebrated. The Italians revived the cosmetic secrets of the ancients, then disseminated this knowledge throughout Europe. By the end of the fifteenth century, a French lady of fashion might use artificial color for her hair, lips, cheeks, eyebrows, eyelids, breasts, and fingernails, as well as depilatories, ointments, oils, soaps, mouthwashes, lotions, creams, night masks, champagne and milk baths, and of course perfumes.

Jean Liébault's *Trois livres de l'embellissement et ornament du corps humain,* published simultaneously in Latin and French at Paris in 1582 and heavily indebted to Giovanni Marinello's *Ornamenti delle donne,* suggested the psychological importance of the cosmetic mask:

> " By the face one knows not only the beauty or ugliness of the entire body but also the customs and affections of the soul, good or bad, ugly or beautiful; in as much as, in the face, all the affections of the soul or of the spirit imprint some sign and significance of their issue, being like the face of a clock; whereupon the hours are marked, the wheels and movements hidden inside. . . . Thus the face is foremost among all parts of the body where beauty, grace, and gentility have their abode. ”[18]

The face, as the reflection of the soul, must be carefully attended, its spiritualism accentuated, "made up." Cosmetics could provide this emphasis. Liébault further suggested healthy living, avoidance of temperature extremes, and keeping both face and chest out of moonlight. His was a mystic art, the face a painting of the soul.

Queen Elizabeth I of England was an avid amateur cosmetician and bought large quantities of cosmetic components from her apothecary, Hugh

Moran. Anxious to preserve a beauty she never really possessed, anxious to maintain an illusion of youth, she masked herself in make-up, perpetuating the cosmetic excess that would linger for centuries. What began as an improvement upon nature became full-fledged artifice. Again the poets were watching the paint show. Hamlet muttered disapprovingly, "I have heard of your painting too, well enough; God has given you one face, and you make yourselves another."[19]

In *Anthropometamorphosis: Man Transformed; Or, the Artificial Changeling*, John Bulwer catalogued the various distortions of the human body, practiced by peoples all over the world. Among these perversions, he noted contemptuously:

> " Verily there are they who do something worth the spight of envious and foule diseases, and invite the hand of God to strike them with deformity; for they set by their false Face more than they do by their true. . . . A wild thing, thus to force and wrong Nature with Bird-lime, Chaulk, Dawbing, and such trash, plainly marring all the beauty they have of Nature, growing foule with making themselves faire. . . . Ere long these adulterate Colours will moulder, and then the old maple-Face appeares, which is sufficiently laught at by all, besides the harm the Paint hath done; for, that Face which was bad enough, is hereby made worse; there being a venemous quality in the paint which wrinkleth the Face before its time. . . . "[20]

A few years later, in 1672, William Salmon, Professor of Physick, published an art manual, *Polygraphice or the Arts of Drawing Limning Painting &c*. After discussing proportion, perspective, use of color, gilding, drawing animals, etc., he spoke "Of Painting of the Face and Skin," recommending that artists apply their various skills to live subjects as well as to canvas:

SIXTEENTH-CENTURY ENGLISH DEVIL, APPLYING COSMETICS.

TWENTIETH-CENTURY FRENCH COSMETICIAN, SKILLED IN THE USE OF MASKS.

"   . . . the Painting of a deformed Face, and the licking over of
an old, withered, wrinkled and weatherbeaten skin, are as
proper appendices to a Painter, as the rectification of his
Errors in a piece of Canvase: Nor is there any reason, but
that the Artist should shew his care in the one, as well as to
expose his skill in the other, since a *single deformity in the
body, begets a complication of miseries in the mind, and a
unity of defects a multiplication of Evils.* . . . *Deformity* is a
disease esteemed the most pernicious, and its issue is a matter
of dangerous consequence, chiefly *obstructions to Ladies
Preferment.* . . . The use of these beautifiers, will make you
as fit for the entertainment of *Courtiers,* as ever you were
before for the courtship of *Grooms* or *Hostlers,* and make your
rusty skins and *ill-look'd faces,* to outshine with a radiant
lustre, the most splendid of all the *Nymphs of Diana.*   "[21]
Cosmetics were the mask of aristocracy, the pale complexions
and smooth skins of women who did not need to work for a living. They allowed a
woman to compete in the marriage market, holding out to her the promise of social
(and consequently financial) advancement.

Salmon's favorite recipe for face paint reads:

"   Take Venetian Talk, cleve it into slices, digest it in the heat
of the Sun, or of a horse-dunghil for a month, with distilled
vinegar, made of Spanish wine, adding every day new distilled
vinegar to the former, till the vinegar be mucilagenous; which
then distill by a luted retort and a large receiver with a naked
fire. First there comes forth the vinegar; then a white oil,
which separate. After you have cleansed the skin . . . then
first wash with the vinegar, after anoint with the oil: if
the face be first well wash'd from all impurity, this one
anointing may hold for a month without fading.   "[22]

31.

Salmon was ancestor to the modern make-up artist, but his ambitions were greater than those of his twentieth-century counterparts. He believed he could paint onto women the faces that their social pretensions demanded, altering reality to suit imagination. It is no wonder then that his book ends with a chapter on alchemy.

Revolution, especially revolution with moral or religious overtones, is probably the only social force capable of controlling the female appetite for cosmetics. In England, the Commonwealth was a time of Puritan bare-facedness, the Restoration one of reactionary cosmetic excess. During the late seventeenth century, Congrevean characters, powdered, puffed and pomaded, played at being aristocracy; and cosmetics were an essential part of the masquerade. Few men dared protest. So it was left for Congreve's Mirabelle to set down the rules of feminine decency that somehow had been forgotten:

> " . . . that you continue to like your own face, as long as I shall: and while it passes current with me, that you endeavour not to new-coin it. To which end, together with all vizards for the day, I prohibit all masks for the night, made of oiled-skins, and I know not what—hogs' bones, hares' gall, pig-water and the marrow of a roasted cat. In short, I forbid all commerce with the gentlewoman in what d'ye call it court.   "[23]

Cosmetic excess reached a peak in the eighteenth century. In 1770, the British Parliament reportedly heard a motion

> "   that all women, whatever age, rank, profession or degree, whether virgins, maids or widows that shall from and after such an Act impose upon, seduce and betray into matrimony, any of his Majesty's subjects, by the scents, paints, cosmetics, washes, artificial teeth, false hair, Spanish wool, iron stays, hoops, high-heeled shoes, bolstered hips, shall incur the penalty of the law in force against witchcraft and the like

32.

misdemeanors and that marriage upon conviction shall stand null and void. "[24]

There was sufficient cause to associate cosmetics with witchcraft. The English had watched their French neighbors become entangled in scandals of the occult. Ladies of the Court of Louis XIV planned and plotted their love lives with extraordinary guile and determination. En masse they sought out cosmetics, love potions, and, as a last resort, poisons to promote love affairs and destroy their rivals or even their own husbands. Witches were the source of these nostrums, and in fact were the only ones willing to cater to the needs of the women at Court, offering them counseling and abortion services as well as paints and powders, love potions as well as beautifying oils. The drugs they mixed were probably no more absurd or dangerous than those provided by legitimate physicians or cosmeticians, but they were mixed and administered under evil influences. Witchcraft was the Church subverted. It provided for those here-and-now needs the Church dismissed or even forbade.

Late in the seventeenth century, French aristocrats had begun dropping like flies—poisoned! The cry went up, and Louis XIV's Lieutenant-General of Police, Gabriel, conducted an astounding inquiry. As a result, several witches were brought to trial, their testimony implicating some of the most powerful women in France, including Louis' own mistress, the Marquise de Montespan.[25] But this prominent clientele insisted they had bought only cosmetics from the witches. To strict moralists this might have implied cosmetics were witchcraft.

Though the British Parliament seemed sensitive to the dangers that accompanied cosmetics, the women were not. The late eighteenth century was an era of cosmetic extravagance in England and France. Fashion had attained totally unmanageable heights and widths. Then, almost mercifully, during the Revolution, fashion became unfashionable. A woman who displayed the face of aristocracy was sure to lose her head, too high a price to pay for the privilege of wearing a mask. But in France as in England, a restored Empire meant more time for and patience with fashion.

33.

Still, beauty was dangerous. Many cosmetics were simply and disastrously white lead paint, which could irritate eyes, roughen skin, emit strange odors, and more decisively, kill. In 1766 Horace Walpole wrote that Lady Fortrose was "at the point of death, killed like Lady Coventry and others, by white lead, of which nothing could break her."[26] The lady knew she was addicted to cosmetics.

No wonder then that dissenting voices began to be raised against the gospel of face-painting. Health was only one concern. Under Victorian influences it became a matter of good taste not to let the make-up show. Industrialism with its concomitant high seriousness made cosmetics seem frivolous. Religious revivals, a new emphasis on morality and respectability, a growing social consciousness, all created an atmosphere in which fashion and fashions in cosmetics were simplified.

Heavy make-up became the province of the prostitute—her badge of office, her defense. Behind the cosmetic mask, she could function with detachment.

In Victorian England, for example, prostitution was often a second calling for the underpaid actress. Having learned to use and apply make-up for public impact—cosmetics were only the most recent in a long line of theatrical masks—the actress would create a cosmetic mask appropriate to her night life. It would be stage make-up for the particular role of prostitute. As such, it was heavy, dramatic, highly visible—in short, an advertisement. Not all actresses were prostitutes, but prostitutes had to be actresses. Little wonder that they adopted the accouterments of the stage.

In at least one case, cosmetics literally became a mask for prostitution and vice. In *The Anti-Society*, Kellow Chesney tells of Mrs. Sarah Rachael Levenson's great success in the beauty-salon business. Madame Rachael, as she styled herself, sold cosmetics to female believers under the label of BEAUTIFUL FOR EVER.

"   But this enterprising woman was much more than a seller of
      paint and powder and ridiculous nostrums; it could be that her
      preposterously priced cosmetics were not even the main source
      of her wealth. It must be remembered that at this period
      the very notion of make-up carried a flavour of impropriety.
      If it was used at all, it was supposed to be invisible—purely
      a means of improving nature—and if worldly society allowed
      older women a certain latitude, any detectable artificialities
      on a girl's face were indecent. The legitimate side of Madame
      Rachael's business was therefore directed mostly toward
      free-spending women, fairly senior and not too straitlaced. . . .
      The discreditable side of the business thrived upon the risqúe
      reputation of the beauty salon.   "
   Chesney continues:

"   The 'house of assignation,' where lovers can meet in secret,
      is an immemorial feature of London life, and it flourished in
      an age when, though women were enjoying new freedom, even
      demi-mondaines often had to be very discreet. The BEAUTIFUL
      FOR EVER enterprise, with its premises for bathing and
      treatment, provided admirable cover, and in fact it had
      something of the character of an eighteenth-century *bagnio*.   "[27]
   In addition to simple prostitution, Mrs. Levenson's cosmetic
house masked a thriving blackmail and jewelry-snatching business.
      The painted-lady morality that equated make-up with
prostitution held sway for many years. Victorian prudery reluctantly gave way to
a less restrictive twentieth-century morality. When wartime austerity was replaced
by the excess of the "Roaring Twenties," cosmetics became the mask of the
emancipated woman. Cosmetics were becoming socially acceptable and relatively
safe. Women could buy in reputable stores what before they had to make at home or

purchase slyly from houses of questionable repute. Make-up was still heavy and artificial, resembling a cloth or canvas mask more nearly than the generosity of Nature, but as technology improved, make-up became lighter, more flexible, and more realistic. Individualized effects could be achieved with a minimum of fuss or artistry.

When sun-tanned skin became popular in the late 1920s, cosmetics were invented to supply what Nature sometimes refused to give. But not until recent years have these tanning gels and creams been perfected. They no longer streak or fade to yellow and green. On the contrary, they look like genuine Miami Beach; and sales have reflected consumer satisfaction with the mask of sun-flushed leisure.

Because make-up is now lighter and more flexible, it can be used to promote that great American fascination with youth. The make-up that once made a woman look older, more showy, now helps her preserve a young, dewy look. Children of the 1950s who could hardly wait to wear lipstick and grow up are now oiling and creaming to stay young.

Today the cosmetic industry is big business. Chemistry and fashion combine with modern manufacturing methods and high-pressure advertising techniques to perpetuate the use of cosmetic masks. Granted, the masks have become transparent—glop has given way to glow—but it is no longer reprehensible to let the make-up show.

The transparency of today's make-up does not invalidate the concept of cosmetics as mask. Both men and women are using cosmetics to look more human, more natural in an age of electronic technology and mass production. They are wearing the cosmetic mask of health. Now that most people work indoors, they relish that outdoor look, while in the seventeenth century working women preferred the paleness of the cloistered rich. Today tanning gels, blushers, lip and eye color are easier to find than sunshine and fresh air. Other "skin treatment" products are used even by those who resist the more visible forms of make-up in

MADAME ROWLEY'S TOILET MASK, 1890.

their attempt to look natural. The old relationship between cosmetics and health has been revived.

It is significant that city dwellers wear more make-up than their rural counterparts. It would seem that cosmetics help compensate psychologically for the one-on-top-of-another conditions of urban life. Make-up functions as a psychological screen, preventing too-close contact. It is something between one face and the next. In addition, city make-up is a protective mask against soot and other forms of pollution.

Among younger people of both sexes, make-up is do-it-yourself personality—like appliquéd bluejeans, an expression of individuality. For this reason, companies that cater to the young package their cosmetics as though they were paints, encouraging artistic experimentation. Paint pots of color for lips, eyes, cheeks. Paint-by-number masks to suit every mood and imagination. Combining the do-it-yourself-art approach with the current emphasis on natural ingredients, these companies offer the young customer both individual expression and an ecology trip.

The health-treatment approach to cosmetics has in turn revived skin-clarifying masks. Beauty masks are nothing new. Early cosmetic compilations included recipes for night masks and mud packs. For example, *The Queen's Royal Cookery*, by Thomas Hall, Free Cook of London, suggested in 1710 the use of the following multipurpose compound:

> "   Take pure white wax four pound, Sperma-ceti two ounces,
> Oil of the greater cold Seeds, cleansed and drawn without
> Fire, and Magistery of Bismuth or Tinglass, of each three
> Drams, Borax and burnt Allom finely powdered, of each half
> a Dram, put them all into a Pipkin, which set in a Kettle of
> hot boiling water, and when they are melted, stir them well
> together, to incorporate them then having wash'd first your
> Gloves in several Waters, and steep them twelve hours in
> Cream, dip them in this Composition wilst it is hot.
> The said Composition is good also to dip Clothes in, and spread

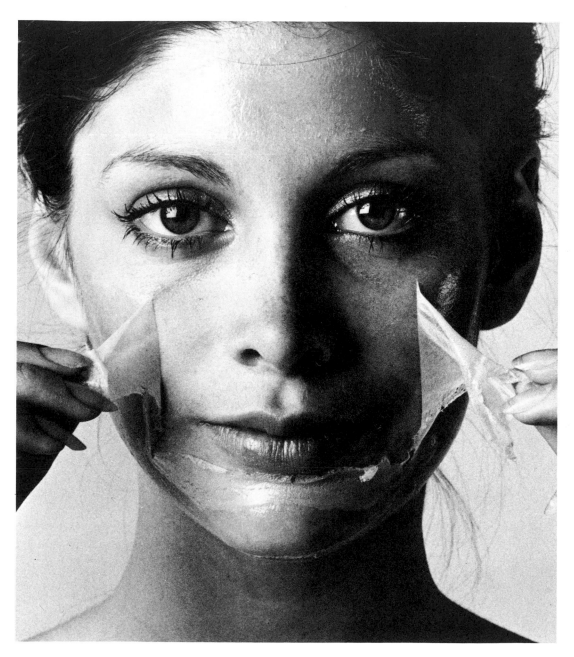

SHISEIDO FACIAL PACK, A PEEL-OFF MASK, 1970.

them for to line Womens Masks; it preserves the Complexion of Ladies: The Ladies in *France*, use it for both. It is also a good Cosmetick, anointing the Face with it at Night, going to Bed, washing it off in the Morning with some Cosmetik Water. "[28] Homemade beauty masks endured. In addition beauty salons offered mask treatments. But the commercial, over-the-counter products are new and seem to be enjoying a considerable success. Their new-found popularity suggests deeper commitment to the beauty ritual, greater belief in the power of cosmetics. Peel-off masks, moisturizing masks, drying masks, cleansing masks, stimulating and toning masks, heating and cooling masks, brightly colored and transparent masks, masques and masks. Whether or not these masks have any lasting result is irrelevant. The point is that women believe in the power of the mask to bring forth the creatures they would be.

Plastic surgery is an extreme in decorative mask-making, or remaking. People dissatisfied with their own faces can opt for a modified mask at a minimal risk. Yet, like all masks, plastic surgery involves elements of the unknown. No plastic surgeon can promise a perfect nose or a flawlessly unwrinkled chin. He can aspire to create a certain mask, but then individual physiology takes over, and what emerges is at best an approximation of the ideal. But men and women are willing to wait and see what surgical skill and their own bodies will produce.

Plastic or reconstructive surgery is as old as warfare and human mutilation. People who destroy will attempt to rebuild. Warlike peoples have almost always been well versed in the surgical sciences. Earliest accounts of nasal reconstruction appear in Hindu medical records dating back to about 2500 B.C. A favorite Moslem punishment for adultery was slicing off the sinner's nose. Other social and moral trespasses invoked similar secular vengeance. Yet alongside of this official torment existed the religious teachings of Sushruta Samhita, who suggested the importance of human salvage. Smite the man with one hand, repair his injuries with the other. The outgrowth of this philosophical ambivalence was surgical competence.

Sushrata described a rhinoplasty in the *Ajurveda* (600 B.C.):

" The careful doctor takes (as a pattern) the head of a plant
the size of the nose, cuts a flap from the cheek according to the
pattern laid upon it, but leaves the flap attached at one place.
He quickly puts the nose in place. After he has incised the
edges he fastens it in the proper position with a good bandage,
carefully inserts two small tubes of appropriate size, elevates
it and strews over it dust of red sandalwood, sweet wood and
antimony. Then he covers it with white cloth and moistens it
often with oil of sesame. . . . When the transplanted flap is
united a pedicle is divided. If the nose is too small one attempts
to make it grow; if it is too large, one reduces it to the proper
size. "[29]

The operation also could be performed by cutting a flap of the skin from the forehead
and twisting it down to form a nose.

Unfortunately, when the educated Hindus came to disdain
manual labor, such operative procedures were no longer performed by physicians.
Instead the caste of potters operated, using clay and mud as nose-adhesives.

Records of such operations also exist for Egyptian, Greek,
and Roman civilizations. During the Middle Ages, classical medical knowledge was
revived in the Italian schools. As in the East, medicine and surgery were separate
sciences. Often it was the surgeon who made the real medical advances, while the
physicians philosophized.

Cosmetic surgery was known to English travelers of the
fourteenth century. Sir John Mandeville wrote in his *Voyages and Adventures:*
"When men pain themselves to alter the body to make it seem fairer than God made
it, they do great sin. For men should not devise nor ask greater beauty than God
hath ordained to be at his birth."[30] Tampering with the mask was inviting the vengeance
of the gods.

But to surgeons under the influence of the Italian Renaissance,

41.

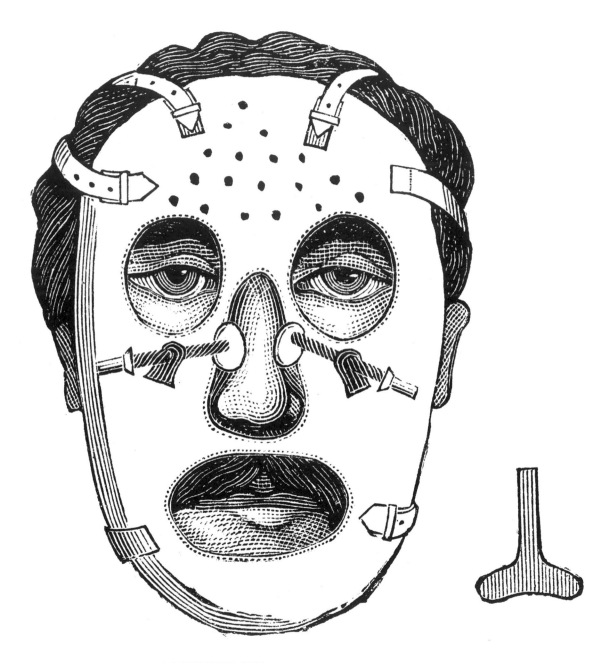

MASK FOR STRAIGHTENING THE NOSE, 1884.

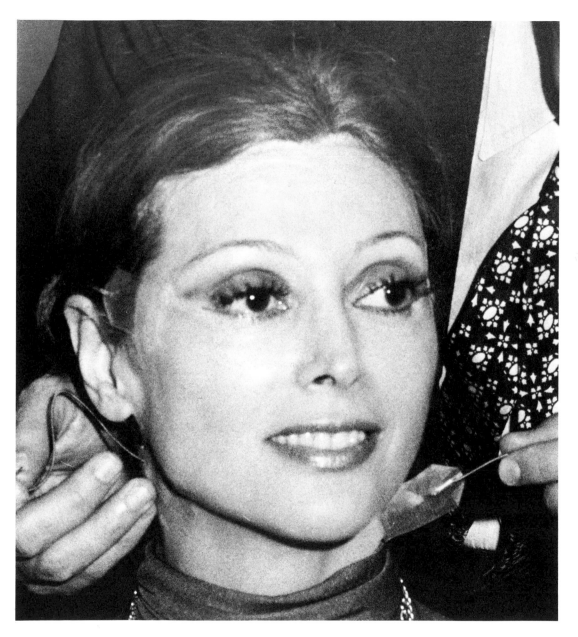

A TEMPORARY FACE LIFT: ADHESIVE, TAPED TO THE FACE AND TIED IN PLACE BY STRINGS THAT RUN AROUND THE BACK OF THE HEAD AND ARE HIDDEN IN THE MODEL'S HAIR, LIFTS SAGGING SKIN.

beauty was god. Gaspar Tagliacozzi further advanced the science of reconstructive surgery, routinely performing rhinoplasties by cutting flesh from the upper arm, fastening it to the face, waiting for it to knit with the skin of the face, then severing it from the arm.

" It is commonly said, that there is much and severe suffering and pain, so that a nose may be fashioned satisfactorily. But they are in great error; indeed the treatment is bearable by the patient so that it conquers every admiration, and that there are more thorny and more difficult ones in the practice of surgery.... Thus noses are refashioned by artificial means, so commendably, that at times nature is surpassed.... "[31]

Though there were written objections in the form of moralizing catalogues to such monstrous alterations of the human body, reconstructive surgery was firmly established, the nose-eroding effects of syphilis alone providing a steady stream of male customers for eighteenth-century surgeons and barber-surgeons. Hackwork was the rule of the day. The new noses might wither and fall off in a few months' time, but desperate individuals were willing to try any remedy at hand. Only in the nineteenth century did surgeons have the good sense to turn back to earlier examples and techniques, thereby achieving more lasting results.

In 1816 Eduard von Graefe described the apparatus required for repairing a nose:

" The patient was made to wear at night a variety of laced waist coat surmounted by a hood. This solidly encompassed the head. Attached to the hood were four or six straps fastened to the sleeves of the donor-arm to accustome the patient as much as possible to keep his arm elevated to his nose. A piece of leather of adequate size was now cut out—usually about six inches long by four wide. This pattern was applied first on the nose, then on the arm close to the nose, so as to gauge exactly

44.

the relations to be kept to each other. The flap was cut on
the anterior, or lateral side of the arm, pointed upward. It
was dissected from above downward so that it remained
pedicled. The nostril margins were refreshed and the flap
applied and sutured by interrupted strands. When union took
place the pedicle was severed at its base from the arm, which
was then set free, and at this base the alae were fashioned
as well as the nares and the columella. The nostrils were
kept open by a small bit of quill, or gum elastic tube.   "[32]

Eventually surgeons discovered that free grafts were feasible. During the world
wars, practical advances were made in the dressing of wounds, bone-grafting, and
tissue culture.

The end products of improved technology are, of course,
more predictable and lasting results. Not just noses, but whole faces, breasts, arms,
legs, hips, thighs—any spot where the skin is loose and saggy, any place where fat
distorts the figure. The surgical techniques developed to rebuild mutilated tissue
now satisfy the promptings of vanity as well.

Dr. Dicran Goulian, a prominent plastic surgeon and head
of the plastic surgery department at Cornell, sees cosmetic surgery as an advancing
trend, a shedding of Victorianism. "Today people who are unhappy with the way
they look have something done, though there is some risk, the amount of risk varying
according to what is being done and who is doing it. A well-trained man won't do
dangerous cosmetic surgery."

To explain the surge in the mask-remaking business, Dr.
Goulian cites several contemporary social situations: the woman who feels her
husband is playing around, the woman courted by a younger man, the professional
woman competing with youth and beauty, male and female models, male homosexuals.
"I am not particularly anxious to do cosmetic surgery on males. A large proportion
of these patients are emotionally peculiar people. The average healthy male bases

social acceptance on other things." Goulian has had male models come to him to change a certain feature for a particular job. The danger here, of course, is that the model can go only so far; then there is no return to the original face.

Today about a half million people undergo cosmetic surgery each year. The more common operations include nose alterations; correction of receding and projecting chins; face, eyelid, and eyebrow lifts; breast enlargement and reduction; alteration of protruding ears; thigh, arm, buttock, and stomach lifts; hair transplants; and acne-scar removal.

Though such operations are performed fairly routinely, the surgeon must be alert to the possibility of psychological complications. If a patient's unhappiness with his or her physical appearance is symptomatic of deep-seated emotional problems, tampering with the mask is opening Pandora's box. The patient will be dissatisfied with the results, demand another operation, sue the physician, or even suffer a mental breakdown. The plastic surgeon is alert to these unpleasant possibilities. He tries to protect both himself and his patient by screening out any prospective client who makes unreasonable demands or who has a history of psychiatric disorder. He will often recommend that a patient consult a psychiatrist before proceeding with treatment. Even for the best-adjusted individuals, an emotional reaction to cosmetic surgery is to be expected: "It's almost a classical syndrome. A week or two after the operation, a woman is emotionally overwhelmed. She'll come to me sobbing, even when she looks good."

As for the actual operations, Harriet La Barre describes their procedures in her book, *Plastic Surgery: Beauty You Can Buy*. For example, the face lift:

> " . . . with the patient under a local or general anaesthetic, the surgeon makes an incision within the hairline at the temple, then down around the front of the earlobe and back up behind the hairline toward the nape. He then separates the facial skin and part of the neck skin from the underlying muscle and tissue, and finally pulls the skin up and back toward the ears.

46.

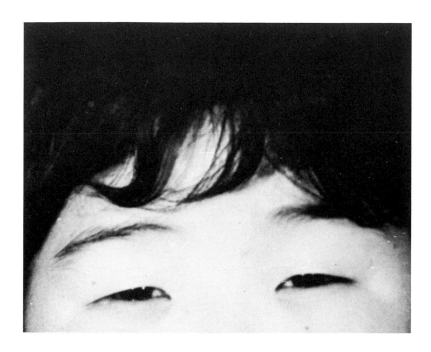

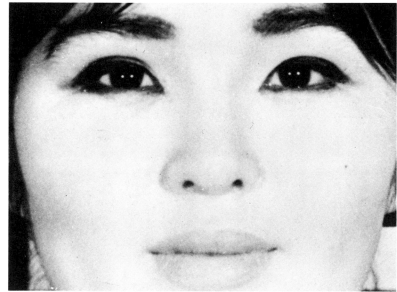

EYE-OPENING OPERATION.

He cuts off the excess skin, sometimes even as much as two inches, and stitches up the incision. Sometimes, depending on the effect he wants to achieve, he will make tiny pleats in the underlying tissue before tightening the skin and stitching the incision closed. Sometimes, if the patient has an unusually fat double chin, the surgeon may prefer to use an outside approach in that area, and will make a small incision under the chin and remove fat and an ellipse of skin. Sometimes, if an obese person has a fat double chin with many crisscross lines, the surgeon may make a longer underjaw incision and remove a considerable amount of skin along with the fat pad. When a patient has an extreme 'turkey wattle' the surgeon may make an underchin cut, sometimes a vertical ellipse, and cut out the considerable amount of loose, sagging skin. "[33]

Frequently a patient will have a minor face lift, then keep returning for more and more drastic work. Once the mask has been altered, satisfaction is illusive.

Though himself a part of this cosmetic extreme, Dr. Goulian does not hesitate to speculate: "There is a strong degenerate theme in our culture. The question is: Can we pull ourselves back up by the bootstraps or will we go down like all the other cultures that lacked motivation?" He is aware of the cause-and-effect relationship between decadence and cosmetic surgery. "This is why the heyday of cosmetic surgery is frightening. The demands are so unreal. Aged women—my god!—who are they trying to attract? The respect for wisdom that comes of experience and requires aging to be fulfilled is lost."

When wisdom and age are no longer respected, the face grows more and more offensive with each passing year. No wonder that in a society where youth and beauty are exalted, hundreds of thousands of men and women are willing to pay and pay dearly to have their face masks reworked to ward away the demons of ugliness and old age.

48.

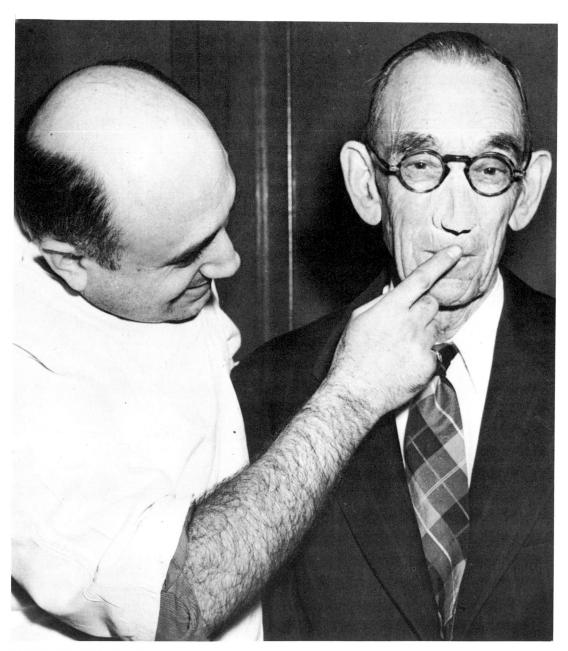

DOCTOR FITTING AN ARTIFICIAL NOSE.

Protective Masks

SUNGLASSES
SAFETY GLASSES
FACE MASK PATENTS
PROTECTIVE VEILS
BATTLE MASKS
FENCING MASKS
SPORTS MASKS
POLICE MASKS
SURGICAL MASKS
RESPIRATORY MASKS
DIVING MASKS
SPACE MASKS

SUNGLASSES: JACQUELINE KENNEDY ONASSIS, 1969.

Protective Masks

Sunglasses are essentially protective masks. The need for protection against sunlight and glare has long been recognized by relatively unsophisticated peoples. For hundreds of years, Eskimos have worn gogglelike shields made of bone or wood with thin slits in them to eliminate snow glare, while allowing the wearer a narrow field of vision. Tibetans have worn eyescreens of a sort, made of woven yak hair, lenseless, but closely resembling eyeglasses in form.

Yet sunglasses are not—nor have they always been—exclusively protective devices. Today, individual wearers consider them part of their social façades. Sunglasses function as decoration for the face while decorating the world, masking it in color. At times, sunglasses have been used as professional symbols— the trademark of the film star or the war hero. Nevertheless, there always was and still is legitimate need for sunglasses as protection; and this must be considered their primary function.

The history of eyeglasses spans several centuries and stretches across two continents. In the West, glass manufacture was an ancient business, beginning in Mesopotamia as early as 2900 B.C. Glass products rapidly became familiar in the Mediterranean Basin. The Romans developed a large glass-manufacturing industry at Alexandria.

The Chinese glass industry developed from these same Mesopotamian roots. Simultaneously, glass was being made by local Eastern craftsmen while glass objects were being imported from the West. In short, glass was available in both East and West for lenses, which were then being used primarily for burning glasses.

The Greeks used glass and rock-crystal lenses interchangeably. Aristophanes referred to a diaphanous stone used to set legal documents on fire; Pliny recorded the use of burning glasses to cauterize wounds. The magnifying properties of certain lenses were also noted. Seneca observed that the tiniest lettering could be magnified and thus made legible with the aid of a water-filled ball of glass. During the Sung dynasty (A.D. 960-112) in China, rock-crystal magnifying lenses were used by judges to decipher legal documents. According to Liu Chi's *Records of Leisure Hours*, judges wore dark glasses of smoky quartz in court to hide their reactions to evidence from litigants.

In the tenth century ibn al-Haytham examined the properties of lenses, primarily biconvex or spherical burning lenses. During the thirteenth century, Robert Grosseteste, John Peckham, and Roger Bacon were experimenting with plano-convex lenses. Bacon went so far as to suggest the possibility of using lenses to improve sight, but the story of his having sent Pope Clement IV a pair of spectacles is doubtful.

Credit for actually making the first pair of spectacles is usually assigned to Salvino degli Armati, who died about 1317, or Alessandro Spina, a Pisan ecclesiast, who died in 1313. On closer scrutiny, it seems neither had anything to do with the original invention. The actual inventor (ca. 1286) was a Pisan layman who kept his methods secret, but was known personally by a friar, Giordano, who mentioned his work in a sermon at Florence in 1306. The earliest written

SUNGLASSES: SUE LYON AS LOLITA, 1966.

reference to spectacles *(roidi da ogli)* appeared in the regulations of the Venetian rock-crystal and glass workers' guild in 1300. The first picture of a man in spectacles was a portrait of Hugh of Provence, painted by Tomasso da Modina at Treviso in 1352.[34]

Eyeglasses, curious devices capable of changing the surface of the world, were quickly transmitted to China, where by the beginning of the fifteenth century, both corrective glass lenses and dark-crystal lenses were being used, depending upon the wearer's intentions—to see more clearly or to be seen not at all.

In Europe, during the Middle Ages, spectacles became popular items, sold in the streets by peddlers. In 1480, Domenico Ghirlandajo painted Saint Jerome seated at a desk from which a pair of spectacles dangled. As a result of this artistic detail, Saint Jerome became the patron saint of the spectacle-makers' guild.

Soon the glass-making centers of Europe—Venice and Nuremberg—were producing quantities of optical glass, the availability of which made spectacles commonplace and led in turn to the invention of the microscope (1590) and the telescope (1608). By the middle of the sixteenth century, optical lenses were also being made for protection against glare. By 1561, green lenses were being manufactured in England. Pilgrims traveling from Germany to Rome wore colored glasses to protect their eyes from the glare of snow.[35] Blue and gray lenses were popular. One formula for light-reducing spectacles involved soaking amber lenses in linseed oil.

As spectacles—shaded, magnifying, and occasionally corrective—became popular, they were put to peculiar uses. In about 1386 Chaucer described a man's poverty as "spectacles . . . thrugh which he may his verray freendes see,"[36] suggesting with tongue-in-cheek naïveté that clear vision was truth. Men who wore spectacles could at least pretend to extraordinary powers of discernment. King Lear advised:

FIELD GLASSES INCORPORATED INTO HEADGEAR FOR SPORTS BROADCASTERS.

> " . . . Get thee glass eyes;
>
> And, like a scurvy politician, seem
>
> To see things thou dost not.   "[37]

Things were no longer what they appeared to be, because that appearance was changed so easily.

> Spectacles themselves were a mark of age, if not dignity:
>
> " . . . The sixth age shifts
>
> Into the lean and slipper'd pantaloon
>
> With spectacles on nose and pouch on side. . . .   "[38]

In Spain gentlemen wore eyeglasses as status symbols, the larger the lenses, the higher the wearer's rank. One Spaniard, Daza de Valdes, wrote a book on practical optometry in which he warned against the use of yellow- and red-tinted glasses, advising instead that greenish lenses "are profitable to sight since this is the color of grasses and plants."[39]

Gradually technical advances were incorporated into eyeglass manufacture. Lens grinding was based more exactly on the physical principles of refracted light; and lenses were developed to correct specific eye failings.

At the beginning of the nineteenth century, most spectacles worn in America were being imported from Europe. The best lenses and frames came from Germany. But William Beecher, a jewelry craftsman, was convinced he could produce better frames to be sold at cheaper prices than the imports. In 1833, he opened a small factory in Southbridge, Massachusetts, to do precisely this. Eventual heir to the business, George Washington Wells, further developed the enterprise, reorganizing it as The American Optical Corporation—in the process acquiring the title of "Henry Ford of the optics industry." When the Civil War curtailed importation of European lenses, American Optical began to manufacture lenses domestically. Later, when World War I halted the European lens supply completely, other corporations went into the optical glass grinding business. Today, such pioneer companies as

IGOR STRAVINSKY, 1959.

American Optical and Bausch & Lomb manufacture a variety of optical equipment, including of course the now ubiquitous sunglasses.

Thus, by the 1920s the facilities for manufacturing spectacles of all kinds were established. But there was as yet no mass demand for sunglasses as distinguished from corrective spectacles. Then the movie industry of the 1930s turned sunglasses into something elegantly decorative. Suddenly, everyone who mattered was wearing them: Katharine Hepburn, Marlene Dietrich, Gloria Swanson, Rudolph Valentino, Greta Garbo, Joan Crawford, Bette Davis. They were playing at privacy while remaining publicly visible. The glasses suggested they had something to hide, gave them an air of mystery and glamour, and put them at one remove from the plebians. A select clique of celebrities, pseudo-celebrities, and celebrity-followers adopted the flimsy ruse of anonymity, posing as harassed, essentially simple folk who had fallen quite mysteriously into a life of relentless glamour. The shaded glasses they wore changed their way of seeing less than it altered the way the public saw them. Rose-tinted lenses were in the eyes of the beholders, as well as the beheld. For the moment, sunglasses were decorative masks.

During World War II sunglasses were perfected as protective devices. In response to reports of freak accidents occurring at night—cases in which pilots reported failure to see approaching enemy aircraft, etc.—a Vision Committee, headed by Dr. R. H. Peckham, was formed to conduct experiments on night vision.[40] The committee found that exposure to bright light and glare during daytime hours could impair night vision 50 per cent or more. The next step was to develop protective glasses for use by pilots and gunners. Polarized glass filtered not only direct light but also refracted rays; gray glass provided maximum protection without distorting natural colors; and only glass would filter out harmful infrared rays. Soon 25 million soldiers were equipped with sunglasses made to these specifications. The sunglasses that war heroes brought home with them were effective protective devices as well as masks of bravery, honor, achievement—an irresistible combination. Sunglasses became an American institution.

GENERAL DOUGLAS MAC ARTHUR AT THE LEYTE FRONT, 1944.

The booming economy of the postwar years gave people the time and the means to follow the sun. Sun tans suddenly became a status symbol, indicating a life of pleasurable leisure. In the process of acquiring their prestigious suntans, millions of individuals discovered the uses of sunglasses. But beyond practical use, sunglasses were seized upon by the expanding fashion industry. Styles in sunglasses began to reflect seasonal fashion shifts. Eyewear ads appeared in magazines. Sunglass boutiques opened in cities across the country. Advertising assured men and women alike that they needed sunglasses to lead complete and stylish lives.

Today in sunlight and shadows, indoors and out, rain and shine, people wear sunglasses as though they were decorative masks. While clear prescription eyeglasses have diminished into contact lenses, sunglasses have grown larger, more evident, more highly styled. Some $25 million is spent on sunglasses each year in the United States alone. In fact, a parasite "funglasses" industry has sprung up to satisfy the demand for stylish glasses that do not necessarily fulfill ophthalmic requirements.

Even the Army acknowledges the importance of fashion in sunglasses. Recently it replaced the outmoded gray spectacle frames with popular black plastic models to enable the serviceman in civilian clothes to blend in more easily. Sunglasses as decorative masks help people adjust to social circumstance. As with cosmetics, sunglasses are more prevalent in cities than in rural areas. Though they may be no more than lightly tinted glass or plastic, they do provide a sense of social distance as well as protection against soot and dust. Darker sunglasses can serve as a real physical disguise, masking at least some of the facial features—from the proverbially embarrassing black eye to the small scars left about the eyes by minor face-lifting operations.

Eyes have long been acknowledged as a reflection of inner emotion. Saint Jerome, who lived from A.D. 342 to 420, never saw a pair of spectacles, but noted the power of the eye to communicate: "The face is the mirror of the mind, and eyes without speaking confess the secrets of the heart."[41] At times what is secret should remain so. Then, sunglasses protect the individual from emotional exposure.

USAF FIGHTER PILOTS WEAR RED-GLASS GOGGLES TO ADAPT THEIR EYES FOR NIGHT PERCEPTION.

Though sunglasses do function in this manner as social façades or decorative masks, no doubt they would not exist today if not essentially practical. Other masks would serve to hide emotion and shield the too-communicative eyes. But no other masks can answer the need to provide real protection for the eyes.

*I*n 1870, Gile J. Willson and his son Thomas set up a company in Pennsylvania to produce spectacle lenses to protect workers' eyes from physical impact. Hiring European lens-grinders, they developed a special glass compound that was impact-resistant. In Chicago, around the turn of the century, an optician complained of the frequency with which he was installing artificial eyes and traced the problem back to the hazards of work in local foundries. He went to American Optical Corporation and suggested they develop safety goggles. Accordingly, they developed heat-tempered, impact-resistant glass for use in a variety of goggles and face shields.

Today, most large optical corporations manufacture masks to protect workers' eyes and faces from flying chips, fiery sparks, splashing chemicals, and ultraviolet rays (from welding torches). Their products include eyeglasses with safety lenses, goggles, helmets with face shields, welders' helmets with windows, and wire-mesh face guards. A variety of safety glasses is used. In addition, synthetic materials have been compounded to meet specific safety hazards. Polycarbonate is an almost indestructible, heat-resistant plastic. Vinyl acetate is especially resistant to corrosive agents. Cellulose acetate protects against foreign particles, impact, sparks, molten metals, and noncorrosive liquids. Most welding masks are now made of fiberglass with tinted windows to shield eyes against infrared rays.

*N*ot only the eyes, but also nose, cheeks, lips, ears can be protected. The records of the United States Patent Office chronicle American inventors' fascination with such protective apparatus. Since the patenting process was formalized in 1790, several thousand face masks have been registered. Some are simple, some complex, most quite ugly, and a few quite cumbersome. All seem to slip quickly into oblivion, suggesting

SUN SHADE.

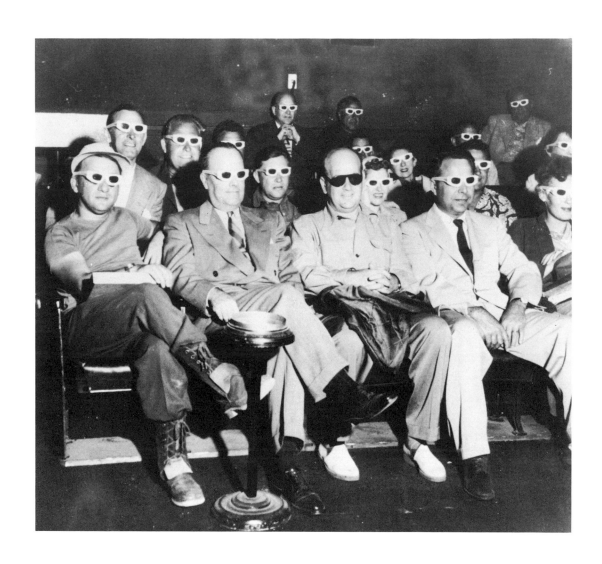

AUDIENCE AT FIRST 3-D MOVIE, 1953.

AUDIENCE AT ATOMIC BOMB TEST, 1955.

BEEKEEPERS, PETER BRUEGHEL (1529?–1569).

perhaps that a protective mask if not entirely necessary must satisfy some aesthetic needs before it can become popular.

Bee tenders began using protective masks of netting in the late nineteenth century when veils were popular fashion accessories. According to one bee-raising expert, John Hunter, who wrote *A Manual for Bee-Keeping* in 1875:

> " Many devices in the shape of Bee dresses, some very ingenious, have been resorted to in order to protect the wearer against being stung; but, as in many other things, the simplest is oftimes best, and nothing more is requisite than a veil and gloves. An economical and very good veil is made of coarse black leno, costing fourpence per yard, made into a bottomless bag, 27 inches by 24 inches. In one end let be run half a yard of elastic, not too strong, which will complete the veil for use. . . . Thus equipped, the aspirant to Bee honours may bid defiance to his angry little friends. "[42]

This simple bag was worn over a wide-brimmed hat. Other more elaborate designs incorporated wire hoops to hold the veil at a greater distance from the face and body, though the principle and certainly the effects remained the same.

Mosquito netting was a protective mask or veil in the days before insect repellents and wire-mesh window screens. People and beds were draped in white cotton netting to keep out mosquitoes and other flying insects.

Sleeping in a bed draped in mosquito netting is a peculiar experience. The netting masks the sleeper in luxurious privacy. The white, billowy fabric is cool, refreshing, almost like sleeping in a cloud. No wonder movie prop men threw mosquito nettings around the beds in every African-safari movie.

Mosquito netting was made up into smaller masks by Horace Harris of Newark, New Jersey, who patented an Improved Mosquito Guard, beneath which a man under insect attack could sleep in peace.

One final note on protective veils: at the turn of the century, motoring veils were worn by women to protect their complexions from the dust blown up into open cars. These emerald-green veils—green was considered the best protection —disappeared along with dirt roads and open cars.

*O*ver the years men have invented certain more substantial protective masks to guard against the injuries that might result from serious or recreational combat. Battle masks are as old as human belligerence. The earliest were used to invoke divine aid or to frighten off the enemy before any damage could be done. Among some primitive tribes, martial masks were thought to be storehouses of energy. In northeastern Liberia, for instance, "ritual required a mask which had proved a failure in battle should be given new vigour by human sacrifice."[43]

Greeks and Romans, at home on the battlefield, wore helmets, some of which were equipped with rigid nose shields. Medieval Norman helmets, cast from a single piece of metal, were conical in shape, the front brim extending down to cover the nose. By the end of the twelfth century, these rigid nose guards were elaborated into full face masks. During the next two centuries, headgear grew in complexity and volume, evolving into large, bucketlike machines, which rested firmly if not securely on the combatants' shoulders and resembled rudimentary diving helmets. These inverted buckets were perforated in front in the shape of a cross to provide openings for eyes, nose, and mouth.

Late-thirteenth-century armor usually included some type of face shield, either chain mail or a visor. Visors were used well into the fifteenth century, gradually taking on more fanciful shapes, finally fashioned as grotesquely featured masks to terrify the enemy.

When battle techniques and weaponry improved, armor became obsolete; it was worn primarily in tournaments. And from the tournament armor fencing masks evolved.

MOTORING VEIL.

*U*ntil the sixteenth century, fencing was practiced only by a select guild of fencing masters, who carefully guarded the secrets of their prowess. But the publication during the sixteenth century of illustrated fencing manuals revealed the secrets to the interested layman. Still a maskless pastime, this polite form of combat was circumscribed by a protocol devised to prevent serious head and body injuries. Though metal practice masks with horizontal eye slits were known in the mid-eighteenth century, there was reluctance on the part of the masters to wear such devices. In June of 1763, Samuel Pepys witnessed his first fencing match: "And here I come and saw the first prize I ever saw in my life, and it was between Matthews, who did best at all weapons, and one Westwicke, who was soundly cut several times in the head and legs that he was all over blood." The situation was fairly common.

Writing in 1892, fencing buff Alfred Hutton described the reluctant adoption of the fencing mask:

> " About the middle of the last century [i.e., 1750], wire fencing masks were introduced, but there was a feeling against them on the part of the masters, and it was some considerable time before they came into general use; previous to their adoption a fencing bout bore a somewhat stately and academic aspect—the movements were slow, and it was a matter of etiquette not to *riposte* until after the adversary had recovered from his lunge for fear of injuring his face. All this, however, was altered about the beginning of this century, when the attitude of the masters toward the mask was changed by a serious accident which happened to one of them, and under the auspices of such men as Jean Louis, Gomard, Cordelois, and others, not to mention many famous teachers of the present day, the art of point-fencing has attained its climax. "[44]

*B*y the end of the nineteenth century, sportsmen in other fields began toying with the idea of protective masks. The first baseball mask, worn by Jim Tyng, captain of the Harvard team, was invented by his teammate Fred Thayer. According to a contemporary newspaper account, "When this new contraption appeared, it was variously referred to as a 'muzzle,' 'rat-trap,' or 'bird-cage,' and one wag remarked, 'We shall probably soon behold the spectacle of a player sculling around the bases with stove-funnels on his legs and boiler-iron riveted across his stomach.' "[45] The prophecy was not fulfilled.

In his book *Football Through the Years*, Dean Hill traces the evolution of the football mask:

> " When intercollegiate football was first played in this country the players wore no equipment to protect against injury other than knitted caps, these being worn more for decoration than to prevent injury to the head. In the early Nineties, shin guards, rubber nose guards, and head helmets made their appearance. . . . The head helmets worn at that time were made of strips of padded leather in contrast to the solid helmets of today. Shin guards and nose guards disappeared along with the mass plays but the helmets were retained because protection for the head and base of the skull was still vital.
>
> Contrasted with the skeleton helmets and rubber nose guards worn in the Nineties, the present-day combination helmet and nose guard is a grim, bellicose contraption. Present-day rules are not as clear as they might be as to the type of combination nose and head helmet that may be used. However, it is only when a player has an injured nose that the combination helmet is substituted for the regulation helmet.   "[46]

Today, masks are worn in fencing, football, baseball, ice hockey, lacrosse, boxing, etc. In all cases, the mask was introduced amidst jeers of "coward" and "pretty-boy" but inevitably became indispensable to the game. No one

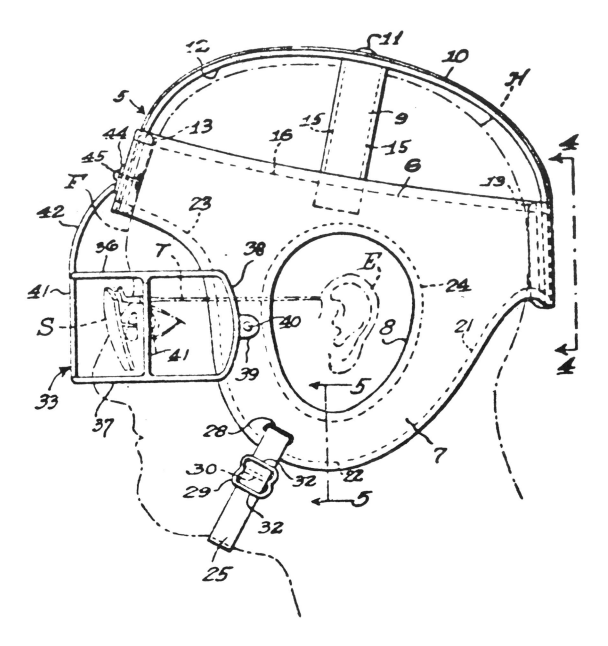

PATENTED SPORTS MASKS.

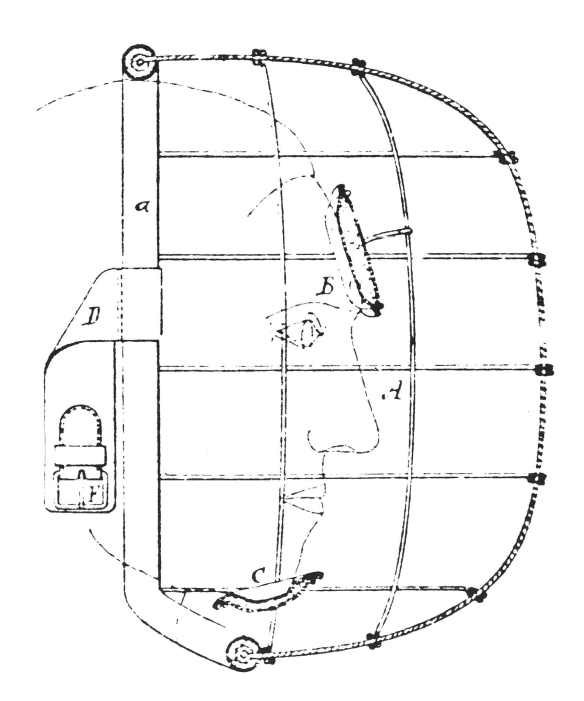

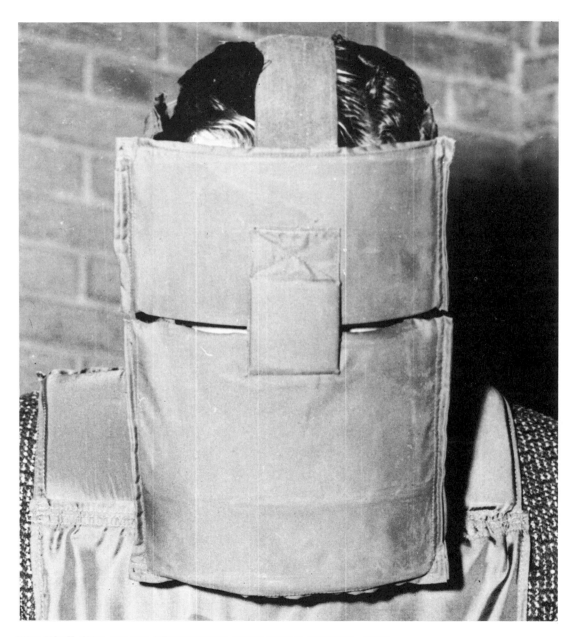

NEW YORK CITY POLICE DEPARTMENT BOMB-SQUAD MEMBER, 1957.

really wants to spoil that irremovable mask, the face. Wearing an artificial protective mask is a fairly obvious and satisfactory alternative.

Police forces throughout the United States and indeed the world also use a variety of protective masks and shields. One police-equipment supply corporation advertises lightweight, shatterproof riot shields made of double-thick, transparent polycarbonate that can withstand the heaviest blows from clubs, rocks, and bottles as well as damage from acids. The shield, carrying the standard police decal, "offers portable protection for police when facing a violent mob," and sells for $49.50. Police helmets with flip-up, transparent windows cost $16.90 in plastic, $19.60 with an aluminum helmet. Motor cyclists often wear helmets with similar flip-up windows. But the *pièce de résistance* is the bomb-squad mask.

Police departments of most large cities in the United States now include bomb squads. When a bomb is discovered, specially trained detectives, shielded in body armor and face masks, remove the object to their bomb van, then haul it to the nearest Army post, where they explode it. The protective mask used by most of the bomb-squad police is manufactured by Federal Laboratories, Inc., of Saltsburg, Pennsylvania. It consists of a plate-metal hood, which covers the head, face, and neck, penetrated only by a narrow viewing slit in the front, the whole resembling an inverted metal wastepaper basket. "Ideal when working with high-explosive devices or for officers who are subjected to gunfire," the complete outfit, consisting of vest, hood, arm and leg protection (large size), sells for $495; the hood alone costs just $65.

Surgical masks, like the battle masks, derive from primitive prototypes. Over the centuries, surgical masks have evolved from the carved, wooden face shields worn by witch doctors while exorcising the demons of disease to the simple, lightweight, gauze, foam, or molded-synthetic-fiber respiratory filters worn by doctors and nurses today.

At the most primitive level, disease itself is a mask that alters the features, sometimes permanently. In Bali and Java, disease masks are used in connection with folk theatricals. The comic characters, rural bumpkin types prone to misfortune, wear masks that seem to reproduce the ravages of familiar yet frightening diseases, such as leprosy.

Just as disease can be a mask, so can it be cured by the use of medicinal masks. The hierarchy of Ceylonese medicine men has attributed all diseases to the malign influence of a storehouse of gods. The Ceylonese beliefs are a peculiar blending of primitivism, Buddhism, and medieval European medicine based on the balance of the humors. Of the many spirits, or yakka, who spread disease, nineteen actually cause illness:

> "   Each of these yakka may cause a certain disease, or rather an indisposition, a disorder, physical or mental, in the person he means to strike. But . . . it is more a question of an indefinable indisposition than of a definite illness such as typhus, dysentery, malaria, or tuberculosis, etc. In all the legends it is related that the yakku concerned has had permission from the highest deity, Sakra, or from Gautama Buddha, to afflict people with diseases, but only on condition that they are restored to health when an offering, combined with the performance of a ceremony, is presented.   "

The ceremony includes a devil dance, in which the witch doctor and his cohorts appear wearing masks that represent those of the nineteen gods responsible for the particular symptoms the patient is suffering.

> "   The illnesses caused by the Kala-sanniya and his associates are, in contrast to the harm due to the other yakku, generally physical in nature. They arise from disturbances of the equilibrium between the three humours, which are usually called sanniya. Very often they are purely physical defects such as blindness, deafness, and paralysis, etc.   "[47]

The nineteen deities, each responsible for one such defect, form a Merck Manual of

78.

Ceylonese ailments. The mask that represents each deity is prescribed treatment for one specific symptom or disease.

Curiously enough, medical masks have been used in a similar fashion as recently as 1858 at Fuchow in China. Five local gods had been held responsible for causing a cholera epidemic; masks representing these gods were made and deposited in paper boats that were floated on the river, then set on fire.

Using masks to exorcise the demons of disease is not a far cry from using face coverings to avoid infection. An illustration from a manuscript in the British Museum depicts King Edward the Confessor (1043–1066) touching a woman for scrofula, tuberculosis of the lymph nodes of the neck. The woman has drawn part of her headdress across her mouth so that it resembles a mask. She may have done so to conceal her bad breath and thus prevent her pestilential vapors from infecting the Court or to cover the ugly, swollen glands characteristic of the disease. In either case, this may be considered a medical mask, worn by the patient rather than the physician, in this case the King.

During the Middle Ages, while academicians associated sickness with the stars, laymen did make elementary connections between disease and the unsanitary conditions here on earth. The prevalence of disease in areas where garbage and filth exuded unbearable odors gave rise to the popular belief that disease was caused, at least in part, by noxious fumes (miasmas).

Royal enactments and borough regulations, passed during various epidemics, forbade unsanitary practices, such as fouling the streets with dead-animal entrails (butchers were notorious polluters) and unloading refuse into the rivers. Some surgeons, who, unlike the philosopher-physicians, practiced more than they preached, did suggest that people avoid polluted streams, infected individuals, cemeteries, and "pestilential airs." Bad or pestilential air included anything that smelled foul, the breath of the sick, breezes that blew in the vicinity of the dead and dying. Because disease was thought to be caused by such vapors and bad odors, preventive medicine was to some extent a matter of masking odors. Aromatic herbs

79.

KING EDWARD THE CONFESSOR (1043–1066) TOUCHING FOR THE KING'S EVIL.

were burned in houses to keep the air free from infection. Wealthy townsmen wore aromatic amulets (*ponum ambre*) to dispel the human stink in the streets and churches. Public perfumers were responsible for improving the odors in popular gathering places.

According to Terence McLaughlin, author of *Dirt*:

> " Many people fumigated their houses, or kept enormous fires burning, to drive the plague away. They burnt incense, juniper, laurel leaves, cypress, pine, balm, rosemary, lavender— anything to cover up the fearful stench in the streets. Plague waters were invented at various times, to pour on handkerchiefs or into pomanders (traditionally a dried orange filled with fragrant oils) for those who had to venture out: the original Eau de Cologne was in fact invented as a specific against plague, and uses a large proportion of oil of rosemary and similar herbal oils with a reputation for healing or prophylaxis. On the other hand, with the curious double-think that afflicts a community faced with a crushing disaster, it was also believed that other *foul* smells could keep away the plague and its attendant reek, and many householders spent their time crouched grotesquely over their privies inhaling the fumes. "[48]

The notions of miasmatic contagion inspired Charles de Lormé, doctor to Louis XIII of France, to devise a special costume that would minimize the possibility of his being infected by his patients and of carrying the infection back to his King. Despite its cumbersome design, the outfit was adopted by the doctors of the French Court. It consisted of a great shirt, or chemise, soaked in a mixture of oils, resins, and powders, over which was worn a coat of Moroccan leather, impervious to "bad air." The head and face were completely enclosed by a hood, fitted with a crystal eye-plate and a nose-container full of garlic, aromatic essences, and rue. During successive plague epidemics, doctors revived the use of this popular outfit. It was last used during the nineteenth-century plague epidemic at Marseilles.[49]

81.

DOCTORS AND ARMY OFFICIALS PREPARED TO TOUR HOSPITALS DURING THE 1918 FLU EPIDEMIC.

More scientific nineteenth-century medical studies, especially those dealing with tuberculosis, brought theories of aerial contagion into focus. In the 1890s doctors began to advise the use of gauze face masks for members of the profession treating people with infectious diseases spread by bacteria-laden droplets from the nose and mouth.

In Japan during an outbreak of Manchurian flu in the winter of 1910, doctors who wore masks remained free from infection. Noting this evidence, physicians recommended the use of masks to prevent infection with a variety of diseases. They sometimes differed as to whether they or their patients should be masked, but, most conceded, the more masks the less chance of disseminating germs. During World War I, experience in military camps and hospitals confirmed these findings.

In 1918, a flu epidemic ravaged the United States. As thousands died and thousands more, still healthy but panicky, voiced their fears that this was really German germ warfare, American cities passed legislation requiring that people in public places wear masks.

In San Francisco, Mayor Rolph published an ordinance, which was to go into effect five days later, requiring everyone to wear a mask. A variety of face masks appeared almost immediately, ranging from simple gauze pads that tied about the head, to the most elaborate nosebags. The *San Francisco Chronicle* commented sarcastically:

> " The police affect the small, serviceable gauze-pad type of mask, resembling in size and contour about nine ordinary slabs of ravioli arranged in a square of three each way. . . .
>
> The Yashmak or harem veil type of mask is used by many girl clerks and women in downtown offices. It hangs loose below the chin and has not such a disturbing and flattening effect upon a certain type of female beauty as has the mask that is tied under the mouth close to the chin.
>
> Hundreds of women have been compromising between the mask

regulations and their dread of uncomeliness by using thick
veils, or the regulation chiffon veils folded to two or more
thicknesses. . . .

When the enforcement of the new order universalizes the use of
masks, fresh and wonderful attempts to blend the arts of beauty
and prophylaxis, and mold them to the form of a mask or a
muzzle, will probably appear, and will afford a wide field for
study to those who feel interested in such departures.   "[50]

Mask slackers were fined as much as $100 or sent to jail for
failure to wear their protective paraphernalia. When the Red Cross ran short of the
proper masks, mask-profiteering became evident. And, finally, the mask ordinance
made law enforcement a problem: a jitney driver, W. S. Tickner, picked up three
masked passengers, who proceded to rob him at gunpoint.

"Did you see what they looked like?"

"Well, they were wearing masks."

So were tens of thousands of other people in San Francisco.

Controversy as to the optimal type and construction of the
surgical face masks survived the epidemic. Variations included layered gauze,
alternating layers of gauze and rubber, a fourteen-karat-gold-filled wire frame covered
with waxed paper, combinations of cellophane and gauze, filters and gauze, cellulose
derivatives, flannel masks, and even paper napkins held on by rubber bands.

Progress in mask-making was temporarily suspended in the
1940s when antibiotics were heralded as a total solution to all problems of infection.
But the panacea proved only partially effective, and in the 1950s interest in surgical
masks was renewed.

Today, gauze masks are worn by traditionalists. Innovators
claim they are inadequate, inefficient when moist, fitting loosely if at all. One
alternative is a molded mask, made of synthetic fibers that filter the air. Army medics,
nurses, doctors, and surgeons have adopted this particular mask. But no matter what

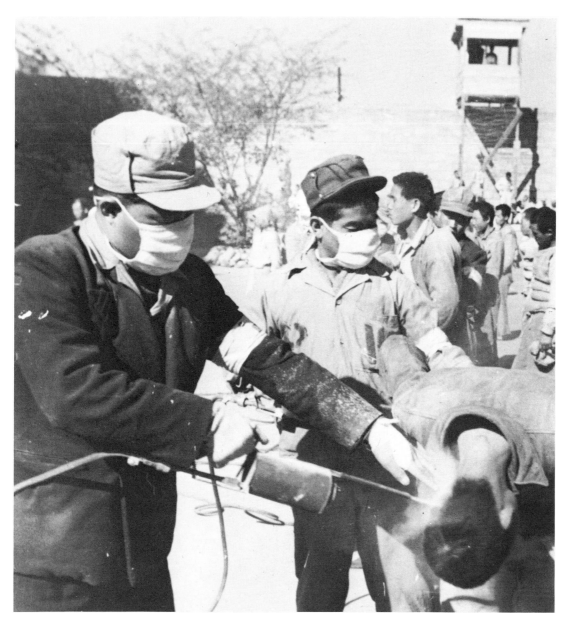

SOUTH KOREAN MEDICAL CORPS SPRAYS PRISONERS WITH DDT, 1950.

POLLUTION MASK, 1904.

the exact configuration of the mask, the protective face covering once worn by witch doctors and deferential peasants, believing in miracle cures, is now standard medical equipment.

Surgical masks are among the simplest respiratory masks, designed to filter, warm, or cool the air we breathe. Today it is not uncommon to see allergy sufferers and other cautious individuals who fear the ill effects of pollution wearing gauze face masks in the streets.

In the days before pollution had become as obvious as it is today, fire and the gases released by fire were the principal respiratory threats. Such gases had been used militarily as early as the fourth century B.C., during the Peloponnesian War, when Spartans burned wood saturated with pitch and sulphur to destroy the Athenian fort and asphyxiate the defenders. Military use of fire and gas persisted. The insidious Italian princes no doubt included fire and gas in their medicine cabinets for treatment of rivals. Leonardo da Vinci advised people under gas and fire siege to place wet cloths over their mouths and nostrils.

When fire-fighting became a profession, firemen, exposed to the dangers of heat, gas, and smoke, recognized the need for protective masks. "It is said that in former days, in some countries, a face-full of whiskers was an essential requirement of every fireman, and that one of his orders at an outbreak of fire was: 'Wet your beard, take it between your teeth, and in you go through the smoke.' "[51] This was a rudimentary fire mask.

Cold air has long been a problem to people with pulmonary afflictions. The simple device of a woolen scarf tied about the nose and mouth warms inhaled air. Setting out conceptually from here, nineteenth-century inventors went to work. Among the more rational of the resulting devices was Julius Jeffreys' ori-nasal respirator, patented in England in 1835:

> " The oral type . . . consisted of a curved framework of light
> material, covering the wearer's mouth and held in place there
> by straps round the neck and by ribbons passing over the top of

the head, and secured either to the hat or to the neck-straps. Pads at the side adjust the apparatus to fit closely to the mouth, while elastic silk aprons follow the outlines of the lips and prevent cold air from being drawn in between the face and the respirator. The inner edges of the mouth aperture are guttered and any moisture collecting there runs off and is absorbed by a small sponge. The front of the respirator is a finely perforated metal plate, behind which are arranged screens of fine and closely spaced vertical metal wire. The ends of these wires are mounted in cardboard—selected as a non-conductor of heat— and all air passing to and from the wearer's mouth is compelled to traverse the very narrow passages left between them. As the wires soon become warm, the inhaled air is also warmed to some extent before reaching the lungs. "[52]

Another inventor, Rooff, used the heat of the expired air contained in a series of valved tubes to warm incoming air. He at least recognized the need to separate inhaled and exhaled air.

A number of camouflaged respiratory masks were also produced, the hardware hidden beneath false beards and mustaches or disguised to look like the wearer's own lips. Masks to heat cold air and to strain out dust from dirty air were commonplace; but a mask that was more than a filter or heater had yet to be invented—a mask that could denature poisonous gases or provide a supply of fresh, breathable air.

Some of the initial attempts to satisfy such requirements were ludicrous. One body mask swathed the wearer from head to knee in leather. A pipe extended from his nose to the lower hem of the outfit. Based on the concept that hot, smoky air rises, the invention allowed a fireman to breathe the cooler air at knee level. Unfortunately, the differential in air quality at head and knee levels was usually insignificant.

POLLUTION MASKS, WORN BY LOS ANGELES MOTORCYCLE MESSENGERS, 1955.

In 1875, Bernard Loeb invented a three-part respiratory headdress consisting of a helmet styled like a bowler hat with a curtain rod running about the rim; an enclosing curtain with a windowlike front portion, covered by a grating and equipped with a windshield wiper, which hung from the rim of the helmet; and a respirator—a filter and smelling essences that could be forced up a tube into the nose. An emergency whistle was enclosed. The design seems not too different from the outfit used by Louis XIII's physician to avoid pestilential airs. Still the most practical of the nineteenth-century fire-fighting masks was Ostberg's air- and water-tight suit, supplied with fresh air from one hose, cooling water from another.

By the end of the nineteenth century a number of filter-type masks, some incorporating chemicals to remove toxic particles from the air, had been devised. But fresh air supplied from a tube was still the only real protection against poisonous fumes. The British firm Denayrouze & Company put on the market a portable patent respirator, which was described in *The Times* (February 18, 1878) as consisting of

" a small tin case of regulator containing the inhaling and exhaling valves, and which is slung at the back of the operator. From the top of the regulator a tube, having a mouth-piece, passes over the operator's shoulder to his mouth, while to the bottom a tube of any desired length is attached, the outer end of which always remains in the atmosphere. The operator also wears a mask, which has an elastic nose clip and lining, and is fitted with glass-covered sight-holes, so that noxious gases can neither affect the eye nor obtain entrance to the lungs through the nose. "

The prospect of even more deadly gas warfare in the twentieth century brought about the invention of more practical and effective gas masks. Tear gas was discovered in Berlin in 1871: a German pharmacist, Graebe, combined

FRENCH GAS MASK, 1882.

chlorine and acetone and the resultant fumes chased him out of his drugstore. But tear gas was relatively volatile—unless it was refrigerated it would vaporize. Much easier to use deadly phosgine instead of tear gas. And indeed the Germans did.

>   "   After the first gas attack in 1915, the necessity for some form of protection became so desperately urgent that there was no time to prepare moulds and other plant for the manufacture of indiarubber masks of the more solid construction, so resort was had to flannel hoods steeped in hyposulphate of soda and glycerine, and to other gas-filtering devices, until a more efficient mask of a pattern which could be made rapidly in great quantity should be produced.   "[53]

On this occasion, Siebe, Gorman and Company produced a mask of impermeable fabric, with noseclip and mouthpiece, connected by a flexible corrugated tube to a canister containing gas absorbents. The mask worked, but was very uncomfortable. In the meantime, the enemy and the other Allied Armies were using more comfortable masks without mouthpiece and noseclip, fashioned from rubberized fabric (U.S.) or grease-saturated leather (German) to conform with the contours of the face. Soon molded rubber masks were standard.

Modern gas masks can be classified according to their air-supply characteristics. Thus, air-filter respirators are used for gas and vapor removal and incorporate either a mechanical particle filter or some gas and vapor absorbent, in a container connected to the facepiece. Combination particulate-removing and gas- and vapor-removing filters protect against inhalation of dust, fumes, mist, fog, and smoke. Continuous-flow, supplied-air respirators are connected by tube to a compressed-air supply. Designed as facepieces or more comfortable hoods, these masks are used in high-contamination situations. Self-contained breathing apparatus permits the wearer to carry his own oxygen supply—either as a compressed gas cylinder or a generative system of solid chemicals which will release oxygen and absorb carbonic acid when moistened by breath. This apparatus is used in fire-fighting or in very corrosive and toxic atmospheres. Each of these masks comes in a wide variety of styles and designs, ranging from the compact and utilitarian to the most cumbersome and absurd.

The Edgewood Arsenal in Maryland, the United States Army chemical warfare center, was established in 1918 as a toxic gas filling site. During World War II, the Arsenal's activities were expanded into all phases of chemical warfare—research, development, testing, procurement, and production. As toxic agents are developed, defensive masks must be devised in case an accident occurs. Some of our most sophisticated gas masks have had their origins at the Arsenal.

The M17A1 Protective Mask provides complete resistance to known chemical agents (including nerve gas), has its own built-in water supply, and permits the wearer to give artificial respiration to unmasked victims of poisonous gas through a special resuscitation tube. The Arsenal's Pine Bluff division, specializing in germ warfare, has adapted a heat-handling suit to their peculiar protective needs by sealing the visor of the air-supplied vinyl hood with silicone cement.

Civilian corporations in the United States also manufacture sophisticated gas weaponry and masks. According to a spokesman for Federal Laboratories (privately owned despite its name):

> " After World War I some farsighted men saw the civilian applications of gas warfare to law enforcement, that is, and set up this company in 1923. We are now the most dominant corporation in the world in the tear-gas field. There are six other important companies and many little guys—fly-by-nights who jumped on our bandwagon. "

Cashing in on civil disobedience and riot-control activities, the company manufactures a variety of gases and gas masks, as well as every sort of battering ram and shield a policeman might ever need.

*D*iving is an ancient trade. Since earliest times, man has sought to extend the

GAS MASKS WORN DURING WORLD WAR I; FROM LEFT: AMERICAN, ENGLISH, FRENCH, GERMAN.

time period during which he can remain submerged.[54] In his *Problemata* (ca. 360 B.C.) Aristotle made a vague mention of a container filled with air that allowed divers to respire under water. Pliny was more specific in his *Historia Naturalis* (A.D. 77), describing a breathing tube used by divers in warfare and working on the principle of the elephant's trunk—the body can remain submerged, air from the surface made available through a trunk, or tube.

Designs for diving masks were included in several early fifteenth-century military treatises. Leonardo da Vinci designed snorkel-like underwater-breathing apparatus, including one complete diving suit. In the sixteenth century, underwater engineers devised a variety of head enclosures, attached by a tube to the surface. Evidently, they did little testing of these devices, or else tested them only at minimal depths, a foot or two below the surface. Otherwise they would have recognized the problems caused by exposing the diver's face through a tube to surface air pressure, and the difficulty involved in forcing air from an area of lesser atmospheric pressure to one of greater pressure.

Toward the end of the seventeenth century, Giovanni Alfonso Borelli came up with a design incorporating a conceptual advance, but he failed to realize this concept in practical terms. In his treatise, *De Montu Animalium*, the Italian mathematician and physicist proposed a self-contained diving apparatus, supposedly capable of regenerating oxygen in expired air. It consisted of a large brass or tin helmet, two feet in diameter, fitted with a circular glass window, the neck fitting into a goatskin diving suit. Exhaled air went from the helmet through a pipe to a bag, where moisture was removed, then returned to the helmet through another pipe. The movement of the air through the pipes cooled by sea water was supposed to render it fit for breathing. It could not possibly have done so. If the apparatus had any success whatsoever, it was due to the limited amount of air that was trapped initially in the moisture bag.

With mechanical realization so far behind intentions, practical diving masks were still of the tube-to-the-surface variety, and, consequently, severely limited in use. In 1754, Dr. Richard Pococke published *Travels in England* in which he described the limited success of such diving gear:

> " I went there (Beaulieu) in order to go to the Needles, to see the curious manner of diveing which they lately began, in order to raise what they could of the wreck of the ————[55] man-of-war, which was lately cast away.
>
> They are let down in a machine made of leather, strengthened at the knees and shoulders, and if I mistake not on the head with brass. There are two leathern tubes to it—one for the air to go down and to speak by, the other to pump up the air. They stay down five minutes. As soon as the man is let down they ask him how he does? and he answers, and they speak to him every minute, and if he does not answer they draw him up; and sometimes, not attending to answer, they have drawn up the man when he was laying hold of some valuable thing. Sometimes, as it is imagined, when they have gone too far down, they have bled at the nose and eyes. "[56]

In 1772, Secur Freminet devised a regenerative-type apparatus similar to Borelli's design. But Freminet happened to include in the reservoir chamber a small bellow intended to keep air circulating. The incorporation of bellows into diving equipment was later to have practical use.

Of the numerous designs patented, some were actually tested and a few showed real merit. In 1802, William Forder designed a diving dress. The upper portion was a copper casing that covered the head and trunk and to which leather sleeves and breeches were attached. The helmet was provided with two eyeglass openings and a place to attach a lamp. It was supplied with air by a tube from a bellows at the surface. Here the bellows concept is appropriately applied, but the bellow was of insufficient force to pressurize the air supply.

William H. James designed the first self-contained diving

96.

U.S. SOLDIER WEARS GAS MASK IN VIETNAM, 1968.

dress, which held a supply of compressed air in a cylindrical iron belt worn by the diver; but the apparatus was never built, so naturally remained untested. The proposed headpiece consisted of a windowed sphere with various pipe fittings.

Finally, in 1819, Augustus Siebe introduced the open diving dress, which set the standards for the entire industry. A metal helmet, to which air was supplied under pressure by means of a force pump at the surface, was attached to a jacket, ending and left open at the waist, where air could escape freely. The suit proved effective at moderate depths, but the open design required some care in bending lest air be trapped within the suit, building up pressure which would endanger the body and prohibit the entry of fresh air.

In 1835, J.R. Campbell patented a similar device but proposed a spherical glass helmet which would provide greater visibility. Unfortunately, glass was easily damaged and the design, therefore, largely impractical. The basic concept of a transparent spherical helmet would be revived for both diving and space masks when stronger materials were developed.

A few years later, Siebe perfected a closed, continuous, airtight diving dress, which operated on the compressed-air principle. The more versatile, though less durable, Rouquayrol-Denayrouze apparatus of 1872 provided air from either a compressed-air tank or a surface pump, passing through a regulator on the diver's back, to a lightweight face mask with eyepieces or a large window set in a metal frame. It was similar in principle to the Denayrouze patent respirator, used in industry.

Credit for the ultimate in diving gear, the self-contained breathing apparatus, belongs finally to the Englishman H.A. Fleuss, who worked in association with Siebe, Gorman and Company. His air-regenerating device, patented as early as 1878, was first employed in mine-rescue work at the Seaham and Kellingham Collieries (1880 and 1882, respectively), then incorporated into a diving dress and when tested in rescue operations the Severn tunnel was flooded in 1882.

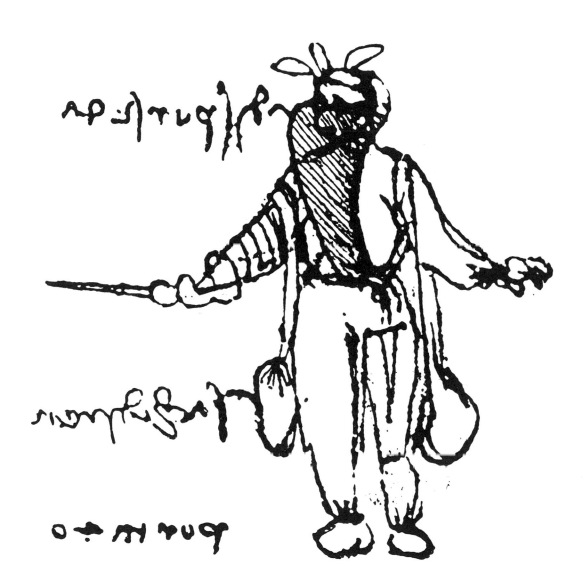

DIVING GEAR, LEONARDO DA VINCI.

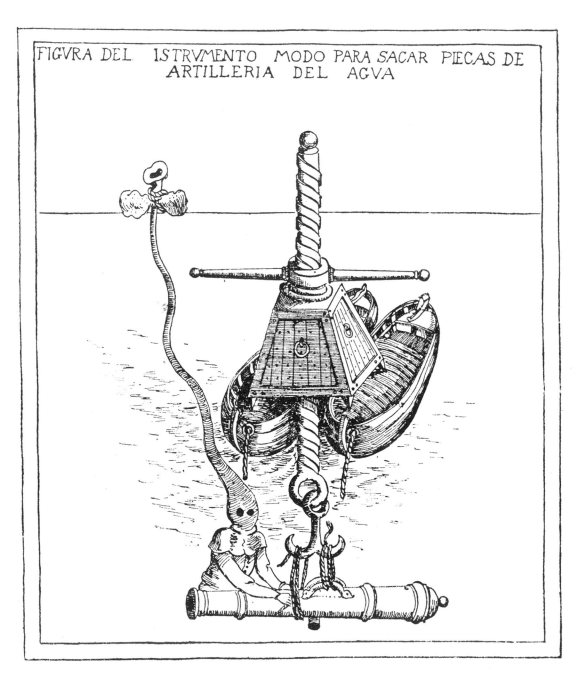

DIVER SALVAGING SUNKEN GUN, 1613.

Interest in the gear was not very keen. Not until World War I did national governments recognize the potential of and need for such protective diving masks. R. H. Davis, who had worked under Fleuss, carried on the effort, applying the improved mask technology to aviation (oxygen-breathing apparatus for airmen flying at great altitudes) and overseeing mass production of self-contained breathing apparatus for British and Allied armies.

According to Davis, Fleuss's famous 1878 self-contained breathing apparatus

> " consisted mainly of a mask of rubber-proofed fabric covering the whole face; a breathing bag and a copper cylinder, charged with oxygen compressed to 30 atmospheres — 450 lbs per square inch, both carried on the back, together with a chamber of CO_2 absorbent, also carried on the back behind the breathing bag. Later, the breathing bag was arranged in front of the wearer. . . . "[57]

Other minor adjustments and stylistic changes were made over the years.

One further development in breathing apparatus was the solid-chemical oxygen-generating system, developed by Siebe, Gorman and Company in the opening years of this century, after they had acquired rights in Oxylithe (invented by Professor Georges Jaubert), a special preparation of sodium peroxide, which when breathed upon, gives off oxygen and absorbs CO_2. Oxylithe provided the air-supply and CO_2 disposal system for self-contained diving suits.

*U*nderwater as on the surface of the earth, man is made a little less dependent upon his immediate environment, a little less in awe of the unknown, a bit more powerful through the use of masks. From the simplest industrial filters to the most complex headgear assemblies, respiratory masks allow man to negotiate the impossible. The air-systems technology that has been developed for industry, warfare, and diving is the means by which we can enter and inhabit alien environments, not only on the earth and beneath the sea, but also in outer space.

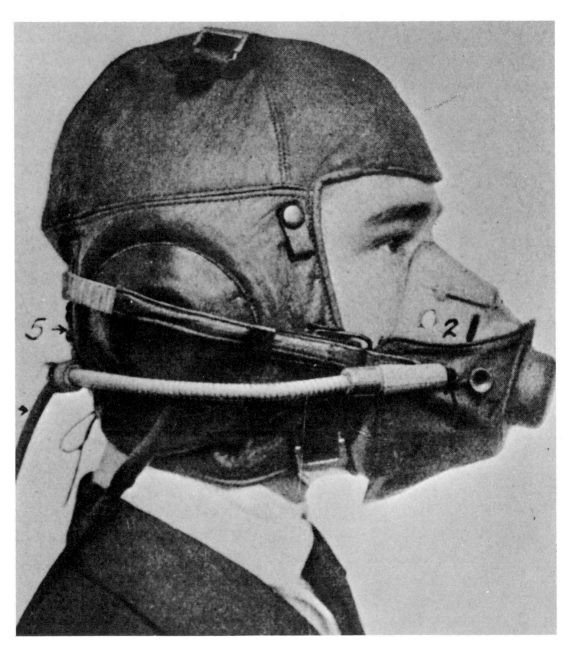

WORLD WAR I STRATOSPHERE FLYING MASK.

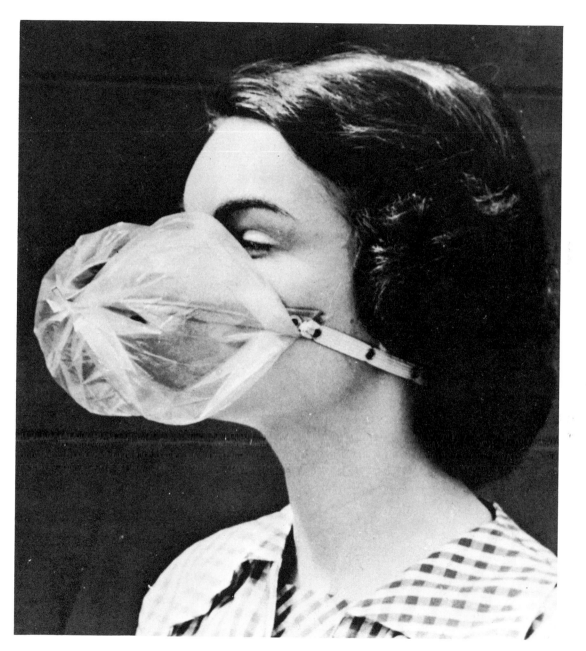

FIRST COMMERCIAL AIRLINE OXYGEN MASK, 1949.

Because of the connection between the various respiratory masks on, under, and above the surface of the earth, it is impossible to say when development of space helmets began. It is known that vast sums of money and a great deal of time have been spent, much of it wasted in the process. In the United States, for example, work done prior to 1964 has been chalked off as money down the drain. A NASA in-house developmental study, completed in 1965, suggested scrapping current space-suit and helmet designs, going back to the original specifications, which had somehow slipped out of the sights and minds of the engineers, and starting afresh. There wasn't much time before the first Apollo manned-space mission. Years of blundering had to be undone.

The basic technology for creating a self-contained breathing system obviously did exist. But engineers involved in development of the gear had never paused to consider the requirements of the various space missions, the tasks to be performed, and the physical capabilities and limitations of the men who would perform them. The air-supply system would work but the masks—both helmet and suit—were inadequate.

NASA enlisted the aid of two young men to consider an alternative design. James H. O'Kane, a mechanical engineer, worked in close association with Robert L. Jones, Ph.D. in clinical psychology, to assess the situation.

Combining their knowledge of men and machines, they set out to test the existing equipment, evaluate its strengths and weaknesses, and then if necessary use what they had learned to redesign the apparatus.

Many versions of the helmet existed. The most feasible had long since been abandoned in favor of the Gemini helmet, according to Jones, "a God-awful Mother of a helmet."

Jones and O'Kane first tested out the existing equipment, and much as they had expected, found it to be totally inadequate for the tasks at hand. Some of the problems with the $25-thousand, seventeen-pound helmet were its weight, which limited head movement and tended to propel the wearer forward in a one-sixth gravity environment; its size, which made exit and entry maneuvers

104.

difficult; the large neck ring it required, which in turn limited shoulder mobility and caused nodding problems; relatively poor ventilation; the need for a bulky movable visor and an accompanying system of seals; the fact that it limited visibility, was uncomfortable, utilized more materials in a complex fashion and so was more susceptible to failure. More succinctly put, "Stupid asses designed this monstrosity and designed it by redesign. Engineers are taught to do this, because, in theory at least, it is cheaper." But here it involved a series of expensive mistakes. Rather than stop something that was running wild, they tried to coax it back on track. These compromises made for an unwieldy helmet, which functioned against its design. "When we began, NASA had no helmet. They had what we call a 'cluge'—some clunker that has been glued and epoxied and latched together. It couldn't possibly work."

After having defined the problems with the old helmet, O'Kane and Jones set out to design a mask that would provide "visual field, impact protection, radiation and glare protection, operational simplicity and reliability, comfort, mobility interface, equipment/spacecraft interface, pressurized feeding/drinking/CO_2 purge/emergency oxygen supply, appropriate eye-heart angle, adequate head ventilation, antifogging of visor, and quick don/doff capability." No small order.

Working with the astronauts, they were able to rethink the uses of the various features of the old helmet. For example, the internal movable visor in part determined the unwieldy size of the old helmet. Removing the visor would mean a considerable reduction in over-all helmet size. So Jones and O'Kane went to the astronauts and asked them why they needed a movable visor.

" The astronauts do not suffer fools easily. They throw you out if you don't know what you're talking about—especially Frank Borman. They told us they liked to have the freedom to lift the visor so they could scratch their faces and pick their noses. We said: 'What if you can take the whole helmet off in a matter of seconds?' They were willing to go along with this. "

105.

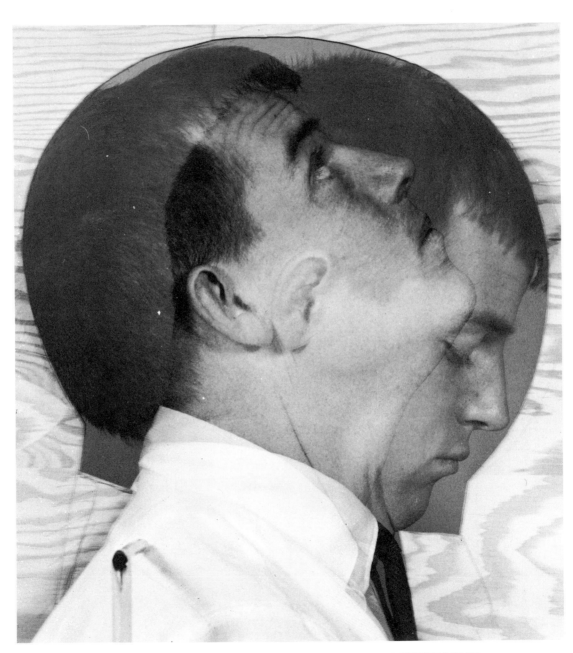

NASA HEAD GEOMETRY STUDY FOR APOLLO SPACE-HELMET DEVELOPMENT PROGRAM.

ASTRONAUT ALAN L. BEAN ON THE MOON, 1969.

Jones and O'Kane did refer back to drawings of medieval helmets for ideas. But more important were their efforts to match task requirements with head mobility patterns by photographing the head going through a series of necessary motions, measuring this minimum geometry of head motion, and thereby determining the shape and dimensions of the helmet.

According to the official study report:

" A one-piece polycarbonate helmet shell was proposed for the functional mockup, even though certain representatives of the helmet industry stated that polycarbonate could not be vacuum-formed to the extent necessary to form a helmet shell. Molds were fabricated and polycarbonate shells were obtained. Off the record, the story is one of masterful one-upmanship. "

Here is Jones's account:

" O'Kane decided polycarbonate was the optimal material from which to make the helmets. Hamilton-Standard, the suit contractors, insisted it couldn't be done. They did a very costly feasibility study proving it was impossible. In the meantime, O'Kane and I made our own model in the shop, then found some adventuresome souls at Lone Star Plastics who would try out the polycarbonate bubbles. They made the prototype helmets, charging us $247 apiece, though the helmets must have cost them closer to $1000 apiece. The Hamilton-Standard people came into NASA to report the impossibility of a design in Lexan, the trade name for polycarbonate. When they came into the conference room, there were our two helmets sitting on the table. "

Needless to say, Hamilton-Standard lost both the helmet and the suit contract. Currently, the helmet is subcontracted out to International Latex.

Today, the astronauts continue to wear the suits and helmets designed by Jones and O'Kane. Minor modifications are constantly being made; but the basic concepts in design have proved workable, reliable, and efficient. The helmet costs and weighs approximately one fourth the amount of the Gemini gear. It can be removed or replaced in three to four seconds. The Lexan outer shell can be replaced for as little as $25. The complete helmet assembly consists of this shell, the neck ring which attaches the headgear to the suit, a feed port, internal head padding, external helmet pad, extravehicular visor assembly, and an internal communications skullcap. The mask provides the protection that space exploration requires, and is engineered to conform with the astronauts' physical and psychological needs. O'Kane and Jones are the most sophisticated of witch doctors, devising the most complex of masks, to protect against the most unlikely of conditions and to put men's minds at ease.

Professional Masks

THE MAN IN THE IRON MASK

KU KLUX KLAN

EXECUTIONERS

BANDITS

UNDERCOVER AGENTS

THE LONE RANGER

COMIC-STRIP CHARACTERS

THEATRICAL MASKS

STAGE MAKE-UP

POLITICAL MASKS

SOCIAL IMAGES

THE MAN IN THE IRON MASK.

Professional Masks

rofessional masks may begin as protective or decorative devices; but their psychological impact soon outweighs their practical or aesthetic importance, and they become the badges of a calling, the tools of a trade. Just as powdered wigs, once the height in fashion, became an official device of the English courts of law, so a variety of masks, once serving some decorative or protective function, are now professional trademarks. This does not mean they have become totally useless, but that they function complexly on a variety of levels to provide social status as well as decoration and protection. These professional masks are the ultimate in modern masking, yet their use is based on the same essential trust in symbols that inspired primitive man to wear a mask.

he Man in the Iron Mask, a late-seventeenth-century figure, was a professional mask-wearer. Because of the peculiar circumstances of his life, his mask was entirely responsible for his social status in his own lifetime and in history.

113.

On November 19, 1703, a prisoner died in the Bastille in Paris. He died suddenly, of natural causes, without removing the black velvet mask he constantly wore. In 1698, when he was brought to the Bastille from the prison of Pignerol, *en masque*, he became an object of speculation. For the thirty-one years at Pignerol he had been in the custody of Saint-Mars, Louis XIV's most trusted jailer.

Rumors of the existence of an inexplicably masked prisoner were at first confined to the Court. Though an occasional aristocrat might be so bold as to ask the King why the prisoner wore a mask, the answers were evasive, and no one was able to learn anything. Then in 1715 a prisoner released from the Bastille, Constantin de Renneville, published *L'Inquisition française, ou Histoire de la Bastille*, in which he mentioned the masked prisoner he had seen. The mystery suddenly became public. Everyone wanted to know who the masked man was and what he had done.

Whispered about, the rumors grew into a masterpiece of gossip, a veritable literary gold mine. Voltaire was one of several who exploited public interest in the masked man. Acquiring his information secondhand from the relatives of those who might have seen the prisoner, he combined what little information he had with romantic elements from the popular literature of the day. He borrowed the iron mask from a novel by Chevalier de Mouhy, and accepted the insinuation of a *roman-à-clef* published in Amsterdam, *Mémoires secrets pour servir á l'histoire de Perse*, that the masked man was the bastard brother of the King. In his own book, *Le Siécle de Louis XIV*, Voltaire suggested the prisoner was the illegitimate son of Anne of Austria, wife of Louis XIII.

The bastard-brother theory gained popularity. Advocates suggested that if Louis XIV were compelled for some possibly embarrassing reason (such as an attempt on the throne) to keep his half brother under lock and key, he would not want the world to know the prisoner's identity. Assuming that a half brother would so resemble the King as to make connection inevitable, one might conclude the mask was necessary, both to save Anne of Austria's reputation and to protect Louis from accusations of cruelty to his own family.

Another popular theory held that the prisoner was Louis' legitimate twin brother, imprisoned lest he claim the throne, again masked because he resembled the King. It does seem unlikely, however, that no one would have noted the double birth at the time of its occurrence, especially since royal births were public occasions, during which the Queen's chambers were open to the entire Court.

Regardless of how flimsy they might have been, the rumors and theories continued to circulate. Everyone was intrigued by the idea of a man who wore a mask.

During the Revolution and in its aftermath of confusion, the few existing records of the Bastille were lost. In 1840, they were discovered in a hole in the floor of an apartment in the Library of the Arsenal in Paris by a young assistant who was repairing his kitchen. This young man, François Ravaisson, devoted the next twenty years of his life to sorting out the records, which included the archives of the Bastille. The archives contained correspondence concerning the masked prisoner—records and instructions that passed among Saint-Mars, chief jailer; the Marquis of Louvois, Minister of War; and Louis XIV.

But these references to the masked prisoner seemed to be intentionally vague—as if participants in the mystery had been instructed to leave no telltale records. Still, the archives did provide a list of prisoners in the Bastille. Since the list of prisoners at Pignerol was a matter of public record, late-nineteenth-century historians, using the rediscovered archives as additional source material, could try to determine which prisoner at Pignerol has been transferred to the Bastille in 1698. He would be the man in the mask.

One prisoner at Pignerol, Mattioli, an Italian intriguer, had been an agent in the haggling back and forth between Louis XIV and Charles, Duke of Mantua, over the purchase of the fortress of Casale. Mattioli, who had betrayed both parties for his own gain, was kidnaped by representatives of the resentful French King, and imprisoned at Pignerol. This much is history. The only possible link between this double agent and the masked man moved to the Bastille was a similarity in the pronunciation of the Italian's name, Mattioli, and the name under which the masked man was buried, Marchioly. But if Louis intended to confuse the public, no doubt the burial name was selected on purpose to implicate Mattioli and thereby weave a more lasting mystery.[58]

The prisoner known as "Eustache Dauger" had also been imprisoned at Pignerol. Eustache Dauger de Cavoye was the son of Marie de Cavoye, wife of a captain in Cardinal Richelieu's musketeers. She had long been friendly with the Cardinal and with King Louis XIII and Queen Anne. When her husband died, she became a lady in waiting to the Queen. Despite her former reputation for being one of the few faithful wives and mothers in the French Court, Marie de Cavoye was known for her wit and grace, and was reputed to be the only woman in the Court who could make Louis XIII smile. In his book *The Man Behind the Mask*, Rupert Furneaux suggests most convincingly that Louis was the father of Marie de Cavoye's errant son, Eustache.

Of the three de Cavoye children, Eustache was the youngest and the black sheep of the family. Educated at Court along with his brothers, he was constantly getting in trouble and associating with unsavory characters. Not the usual peccadillos of gambling and women, but a more peculiar indulgence in black magic and witchcraft. For example, Eustache attended a black mass conducted in the chapel of the Castle of Roissy in 1659.

It is known that the ladies of the Court were involved in witchcraft throughout the years of Louis XIV's reign. In 1668 Le Sage, a sorcerer, and his apprentice, Abbé Mariette, were arrested and brought to trial. Their testimony, implicating several notable women of the Court, including the Marquise de Montespan, was brought to the attention of the King, who ordered the records suppressed. Duvivier, a French historian, identified Dauger with the surgeon d'Auger who participated in this underworld of witchcraft. In 1669, Eustache Dauger de Cavoye disappeared entirely from Court. A prisoner, Eustache Dauger, was entered on the rolls at Pignerol.

If Eustache was arrested for his involvement with the witches, was he the man in the mask, and, if so, why the mask? Why should his punishment

116.

be kept secret when higher ranking men and women were being imprisoned and executed publicly for their participation?

But suppose Dauger was both Louis XIII's bastard son by Marie de Cavoye and the man who had lent himself to the uses of black magic. Suppose he bore so great a resemblance to Louis XIV or that his blood contained enough of the royal strain that he might be used as a voodoo doll upon which a sorcerer might work the magic intended for the King. Then a mask would be necessary if Dauger was in the company of known or suspected sorcerers.

Among those in the Bastille suspected of or known to be sorcerers, the Comte de Lauzun, one of Dauger's childhood friends, had been on intimate terms with the King's mistress, Madame de Montespan, who had promised to secure for him the position of Grand Master of the Artillery. Yet de Lauzun had suspected she would instead use her influence to block his appointment. Secreting himself beneath her bed, he overheard her conversation with Louis, and then confronted her with first-hand evidence of her treachery, repeating their conversation to her word for word. He was imprisoned, finally, for threatening her life. Madame de Montespan, herself involved in black magic, referred to de Lauzun in no uncertain terms as a devil. Perhaps she meant precisely that—he was a high priest of black religion.

If such was the case, and de Lauzun was still seeking revenge upon the King and his mistress, Dauger was material upon which to work out this revenge. No wonder then that Saint-Mars was under strict instruction to isolate the masked man from all prisoners, especially de Lauzun. No wonder Dauger was required to wear a mask when in sight of such men.

Eustache Dauger died in 1703. No doubt the King was relieved. This bastard brother might have lent himself to black magic, becoming the mask through which evil could be invoked and ill fate summoned down upon the King. The mask Dauger was forced to wear in punishment was a constant reminder of the way in which he had abused the power of mimicry. But more than this, it was intended to allay the powers of darkness—to cancel out the mask that was his face.

*I*n 1866, six well-educated young men from "good" families got together in Pulaski, Tennessee, to form a recreational club, which they named after the Greek word for circle, *kuklos*. This first Ku Klux Klan was an elaborate fraternal masquerade. Attired in white masks and cloaks, the members rode about on horseback late at night, played pranks, and tried to scare the neighborhood blacks. The masks lent overgrown schoolboys the anonymity with which to realize their juvenile fantasies. But the night-riding method and regalia were soon put to more formidable uses. As the Ku Klux Klan evolved from post-adolescent trickery to political organization, the club regalia became a professional mask.

During Reconstruction, vigilante groups were formed in the southern states to take the law into their own hands. These groups, led by Confederate General Nathan Bedford Forrest, gradually coalesced under the mask of the KKK. They held themselves to be defenders of the South, preserving its integrity against northern carpetbaggers, Yankee schoolteachers, and judges. Their white masks and robes were supposed to symbolize the purity of their cause.

But the motives of the members of the Klan were far from spotless. Poor whites, at the mercy of the system, they banded together in self-defense, afraid of the newly freed slaves and the larger political forces that seemed to threaten their habitual modes of being. With at least the tacit support of the majority of southern whites, they themselves became a considerable political force, the radical outcropping of the Democratic party, capable of inflicting violence upon their opposition, and imposing a reign of terror which has endured intermittently for over a century.

According to Allen W. Trelease, author of *White Terror*, an extensive social study of the Klan:

> " Booker T. Washington once said that the white man could never hold the black man in a ditch without getting in the ditch with him. The Ku Klux Klan was a perfect illustration of that proposition. Beginning as a social fraternity devoted to playing

KU KLUX KLAN, 1868.

pranks, it was soon transformed into a terrorist organization aimed at the preservation of white supremacy. And in the context of Reconstruction politics after 1867, it became a counterrevolutionary device to combat the Republican party and Congressional Reconstruction policy in the South. For more than four years, it whipped, shot, hanged, robbed, raped, and otherwise outraged Negroes and Republicans across the South in the name of preserving white civilization. "[59]

The old-fashioned fun-lovers retreated from the ranks of the Klan. In 1869, Forrest, appalled by the way the organization had got out of hand, ordered the Klan disbanded. But this did not end Klan activities; on the contrary, the Klan became a full-blooded terrorist organization, waging guerrilla warfare against the Republican party until the Democrats were returned to power and the Southerners again controlled the South. In the meantime, in 1871, Congress, under pressure of public outrage, acted to halt the intimidation, whipping, and murder. The Ku Klux Act made it a federal offense to conspire or go about disguised in order to deprive persons of their constitutional rights or protection under the law. Enforcement of the Act chased the Klan underground, and the resultant ritualized secrecy, which included disguises, gave the Klan renewed strength. Masks reinforced the feeling of conspiracy, set members apart from the black riffraff they abhorred, and allowed them Halloween license to break the law.

Klan regalia began as a white mask with holes for eyes and nose, a white conical cardboard hat (of the dunce's cap variety) and a long, flowing robe, usually made from a bedsheet. Then colors were added, and the headdress occasionally assumed grotesque forms, featuring horns, beards, tongues, etc. But in the long run, the simpler attire prevailed, being easier to put on and take off and to hide when the Klan was outlawed.

The costume did create a carnival air and pranks remained part of the Klansman's stock in trade:

KU KLUX KLAN, 1949.

" Occasionally ghostlike creatures ranging up to twelve feet in height were seen walking the streets or riding through the countryside. This effect was created by means of a framework resting on a man's shoulders, the whole covered with a gown or robe and surmounted by a false head made from a gourd or pumpkin, sometimes carved like a jack-o'-lantern, with a candle burning inside. The head was commonly fastened to the end of a pole; when the pole was raised it appeared as if the specter's neck were stretching. Sometimes a Klansman so outfitted would approach a Negro and ask him to hold his head for a minute as a favor. When the allegedly quaking Negro complied, the Ku Klux would either gallop off or, more economically, wait a moment, reclaim and replace his head with profuse thanks, and then depart. "[60]

When Reconstruction ended, the worst of the Klan outrages disappeared; but the Klan remained dormant, waiting for a leader and the revival of their cause.

William Joseph Simmons was a Methodist circuit rider, traveling salesman, and promoter *par excellence*. In 1915, he espoused the Ku-Klux cause and set out to engineer the revival of sleeping gods. The second coming, complete with ceremonial cross-burning, was staged at the top of Stone Mountain. Simmons then hired publicity agents and fund raisers Edward Y. Clarke and Mrs. Elizabeth Taylor, formed a publicity association, and launched a full-scale promotional campaign. The Klan became the largest, most powerful vigilante group in American history. Any pure, patriotic, native-born white Protestant American over eighteen years of age could join for a mere $16.50. This time around, the Klan was a corporation, Klansmanship an avocation for the average member, a profession for the Klan official.

Simmons' timing was perfect. World War I hysteria fed his cause. The Klan became an outlet for overzealous patriots, do-gooders appalled by evil on a global scale, and men who felt justice was undermined by leniency. By the mid-1920s the Klan had some 3 million members and was again a political force to be reckoned with.

The Klan continued to grow, expanding its litany of prejudice to include Catholics, Jews, foreigners, and organized labor, its membership peaking at between 4 and 5 million in the late 1920s. Then the Depression, corruption, power plays, and public reaction against Klan violence resulted in its rapid decline. Their unwise association with the German-American Bund was revealed in 1939. In 1944 government action against the Klan for back taxes resulted in its official dissolution.

But the enactment and enforcement of civil-rights legislation in the South during the 1950s and 1960s were a loud, clear call to battle. The Klan rallied once more around their tattered flag of racism, hatred, and bigotry. The white sheets and masks were hauled out of storage, and violence rode again.

In recent years, the Klan has endured moments of Federal suppression, punctuated by triumphant, if temporary, returns to power. The current Imperial Wizard, Robert Shelton, possesses the great organizational ability that throughout the years has kept the order alive. Despite periodic jailing of its leaders, the Klan continues to recruit, to play upon the fears of the little white man.

Because each resurgence of fear and insecurity breathes new life into the Klan, the peculiar white masks, cloaks, and hoods persist—a recurrent image in American history, symbolizing the professionalization of prejudice, the incorporation of bigotry.

*M*asks seem to be characteristic of professions that routinely employ physical violence. For example, many of the early European executioners customarily wore masks.

At times the disguise provided physical protection:
" The hangman in Ireland wore a grotesque mask on his face, and was otherwise disguised in a most fantastic manner. On his back was an enormous hump, formed by a concealed wooden

123.

bowl, on which he received the shower of stones that poured on him the moment the cart drew away from under the culprit's feet. "[61]

Given the constant strife between Irish subjects and British overlords, many of the so-called culprits condemned to death were probably popular heroes. The man who carried out the letter of English law had best remain anonymous if he wished to remain alive.

Reprisals against the hangman were a constant threat. He was the vulnerable arm of justice, while the courts, judges, tyrants, and kings remained beyond the reach of the man who might sympathize with the criminal. The mask protected the executioner's anonymity and therefore his life.

As an Instrument of Justice, the executioner was to function impartially—not as a human being taking vengeance on a wrong-doer, but as a machine of State, doling out fair and deliberate judgment. The mask he wore hid his humanity, made him a faceless agent of the State.

Dealing in death could stigmatize a man and his family. The executioner's mask kept his neighbors from knowing him as death's cohort (or at least from seeing him in the role), thus making it easier for him and his family to deal with merchants, peddlers, and friends. In short, the executioner's mask was a practical tradition, rooted in both physical and psychological needs.

But professionalism altered tradition. As public executions became popular entertainment, the executioner was recognized, if not as an artist, then certainly as circus master. Off came his mask. He now sought recognition and approval. The mask was not eliminated, however. It was given over to the victim— to keep him calm during the entertainment and to hide his unseemly, pain-racked face from the audience of pleasure-seekers. Handkerchiefs were commonly used by prisoners to cover their eyes and occasionally their humiliation. Sir Walter Raleigh refused to be blindfolded at his own execution, saying: "Think you I fear the shadow of the axe, when I fear not the axe itself?"[62]

124.

FOURTEENTH-CENTURY FRENCH HANGMAN.

It became routine to place over the condemned man's head a white nightcap which could be pulled down to cover his face. Hangmen prided themselves on adeptly pulling the cap down over the victim's face at the most dramatic moment.

*I*t seems ironic that some of the men condemned to wear a mask at their own executions used masks in their professional callings.

The masked outlaw is a relatively modern phenomenon, conceived in social upheaval, appearing at times of dearth and famine, and in the confused aftermath of war, when rootlessness, landlessness, and dispossession combine with personal courage and persistent individualism as driving forces. The Middle Ages, a time when each man had his niche, knew little banditry. Banditry demanded mobility. So it was not until the fifteenth and sixteenth centuries that outlaws first became a significant social force, and not until the sixteenth century that bandits adopted masks. The masks which were being worn as fashion accessories at this time may have suggested to the would-be thief a more practical use for packaged anonymity. Certainly, masks intimated style; and, if nothing else, the highwayman was a stylish figure in European society.

Historians have amassed a good deal of evidence that the English highwayman was not a lower-class vagabond, but rather a well-bred individual pressed for ready cash or determined to maintain a life style he could not afford legitimately. Civil war and Commonwealth had spelled the ruin of many a Royalist. Some of these gentlemen, deprived of their lands and incomes, took to the roads to seek their fortunes and avenge their King. Young men who had gambled away their inheritances also turned to armed robbery for a living. Liveried servants, tired of attiring themselves in someone else's wealth, sought a bit of their own. Both the lack of organized police and the poor condition of most roads made the highwayman's avocation all the more feasible.

HANGING OF JAPANESE WAR CRIMINALS BY THE BRITISH, 1946.

Because this form of robbery was often an avocation—a second calling for ruined gentlemen—it demanded a disguise. Many a "gentleman" robbed at night the very people he entertained during the day. Others, celebrities in their own time, hid from their jealous fellow thieves, who cared more about collecting bounties than preserving the faith. Defoe's Moll Flanders, the queen of fictional highwaywomen, explained: "One of the greatest dangers I was now in, was that I was too well known among the trade, and some of them whose hatred was owing rather to envy than any injury I had done them, began to be angry that I should always escape when they were always catched and hurried to Newgate."

Prompted by such fears, highwaymen could be quite ingenious in their use of masks.

> " The sixteenth-century highwayman Gamaliel Ratsey, the son of a Lincolnshire squire, wore a mask on which were depicted such frighteningly hideous features that his pistol and sword were almost superfluous. . . . William Page, who was executed in 1758, trained himself to be an expert cartographer, and was found to possess detailed maps, all drawn by himself, of every road within twenty miles of London. He went out to rob in a phaeton and pair which he would leave close by his chosen place of ambush; and after his robbery he would return, remove his mask, change his clothes and his wig, and ride home at leisure. Some highwaymen robbed in disguise: Jack Collet as a bishop with four or five companions dressed as his servants and chaplain; Tom Royland and Thomas Sympson as women. "[63]

The highwaywoman Mary Firth, or Moll Cutpurse, disguised herself as a man and accumulated considerable wealth in her adventuresome calling.

Colonel Blood, who had lost his Irish property at the time of the Restoration because of his Cromwellian sympathies, attempted to steal the Crown from the Tower of London in 1671 in what may have been part of a conspiracy to take over the government. He did so in the garb of a priest, ingratiating himself into the keeper's favor, going so far as to arrange for the marriage of his nephew with the keeper's daughter, then seizing the first opportunity to rob the Tower jewels:

> " When daring Blood, his rent to have regained,
> Upon the English diadem distrained,
> He chose the cassock, surcingle, and gown,
> The fittest mask of one that robs the crown.   "[64]

He was seized as he tried to escape. A short time later, in a personal interview with Charles II, he managed to talk himself back into royal favor. One biographer explained:

> " To gain information of the feelings of the dissenting bodies, and discover what terms would be mose acceptable to them, to track down and bring in the fierce and desperate men from whom trouble might be anticipated, to discover if possible the connection that existed between the sects and those in high places—these were objects of highest importance. They needed such a man as Blood. And it seemed worth while to Charles to tame this fierce bird of prey to his service to achieve such ends as he contemplated. Some such thought evidently occurred to the King during the examination. 'What,' he is said to have asked bluntly at its close, 'What if I should give you your life?' Blood's reply is almost epic, 'I would endeavor to deserve it.'   "[65]

And apparently he did. He was eventually appointed head of the King's secret service, forever to wear the mask of the double agent.

Francis Jackson had devoted himself to gallant gaming and a life of extravagance. He turned to the highway to support a prostitute he had inherited from a friend, and soon became proficient in the use of disguises. He explained:

129.

"	In the first place, you must have variety of Periwigs planted in your Lodgings; and the like you must carry abroad, if occasion require the necessity of changing the colour of the hair; neither must you be without false beards of several colours; for want of them, you may only cross your locks athwart your mouth, which is a good disguise. Patches contribute much thereto. And least your Voice should be known another time by him that is robbed, put into your mouth a Pebble, or any such like thing, which will alter your tone advantageously to your purpose.	"[66]

The use of masks and of disguises as masks by these highwaymen allowed them to feel secure enough to indulge in a bit of gallantry. English highwaymen, as distinguished from the common, unmasked brigands of Europe, were known for their gentlemanly manners. Many were gentlemen by birth and so knew how to treat the people they robbed. Others played up the Romantic notion of the gallant outlaw, seeing themselves as real-life Robin Hoods, enjoying the democracy of their contacts with all manner of men. But,

"	polite and gracious as a highwayman might seem, in fact, travellers agreed that he only remained so as long as his demands were met. Argue with him, insult him, keep him waiting on the open, dangerous highway with his pistol in his hand and his black mask over his face, and you would soon recognize that a very different character lay beneath his manner and the flamboyance of his gallantry.	"[67]

The masked highwayman continued to harass travelers to and from London until the late eighteenth century when the brothers Fielding set up their Horse Patrol. The establishment of a regular highway patrol in the early nineteenth century virtually eliminated the highwayman from the catalogue of English criminals.

But the career of the masked outlaw had just begun. In America, the West was rife with adventurers turned outlaw, anxious to possess the gold that others prospected. Stagecoach holdups were frequent in the mining regions. "Road agents," working singly or in gangs, masked and on horseback, would ambush the stagecoaches, bring them to a halt, and demand that the driver throw down the strongbox, which often contained a small fortune in gold.

Some of these robbers modeled their behavior on that of their English predecessors. But the masks were more hopespun. The neat, little black silk masks that fashionable ladies had worn were now part of ancient history, and certainly not available to the outlaw. Miners and factory workers habitually wore red bandanas tied across their mouths and noses to prevent inhalation of dust. The outlaws were quick to adopt so readily available and attractive a disguise.

But red bandanas were not the only masks used by the highwaymen of the West. Black Bart wore a flour sack with eyeholes pierced through the front and a derby hat underneath when robbing the Wells Fargo stagecoaches in California between 1875 and 1883. It not only masked his face, but also deluded people as to his height. He left scraps of pathetic poetry at the scenes of his crimes, was gallant to the ladies and courteous to the gentlemen. "Not once had he fired a shot; in every case his steadily aimed gun and blankly resolute flour-sack visage had been sufficient to make it understood that he meant what he said."[68] Black Bart was eventually discovered (by means of the laundry mark on one of his handkerchiefs lost at the scene of a holdup) to be C.E. Bolton, alias Charley Boles, a small, balding man with a gray mustache, who habitually wore derby hats and lived the life of a gentleman in San Francisco.

Nor were the frontier bandits limited geographically to the American West. The Australian bandit Ned Kelly wore one of the most distinguished of disguises. Clad from head to toe in homemade armor, he frightened his victims while remaining conveniently faceless and bulletproof. He was finally caught when a bullet passed through a small chink in his armor, wounding him in the knee.

131.

Curiously enough, his outfit resembled that worn today by police bomb squads in America.

Today the wearing of the mask is no longer restricted to the gentleman-outlaw. Rather, it is the practice of the trade in general. Improved police methods have made it necessary for the outlaw to hide his identity. Once his face is known, he hasn't a chance of escape. His photograph or a drawing of his face is distributed across the nation, to newspapers, post offices, and police departments, as well as being broadcast on television.

The masks worn by outlaws today are usually commercial products—Halloween masks, ski masks, surgical masks, and so on. The nylon-stocking mask is a twentieth-century innovation, simple but effective, masking the features while providing an appearance so grotesque as to frighten the victims into compliance. This is a favorite with sex maniacs.

Because so many outlaws are wearing masks, and because television Westerns and cops-and-robbers movies have reinforced the impression that a thief must wear a mask, the masked outlaw has become a contemporary cliché. Masks are one more piece of professional equipment.

With bandits running about in masks and disguises, law-enforcement officers, in order to share in the fun and keep up with the criminal escapades, have also adopted masks and disguises. More and more undercover police, dressed as casual passers-by, chosen for their expressionless, even naïve faces, have been assigned to vice-squad duty and detective work. At times male police will dress in drag to attract sexual perverts or muggers who prey on shapeless old ladies. In New York City, female police recently have taken to posing as prostitutes and applying for massage-parlor jobs.

Masquerades are also common practice among federal law-enforcement agencies. After all, espionage is a matter of wearing a false identity or mask that will allow the wearer access to state secrets. Counterespionage is a mask

132.

LOAN SHARK VICTIM TESTIFIES BEFORE SENATE SUBCOMMITTEE, 1968.

PROTESTANT VIGILANTES, BELFAST, IRELAND, 1972.

of double thickness. Professional spies and FBI agents, petty criminals and local police, must vary their appearances to avoid becoming trade celebrities. Whenever it is to a man's advantage not to be known by sight, the mask, in whatever form, is a professional tool.

*M*asks have become so much a part of the everyday struggle to establish law and order that they can lend even fictional characters a certain reality. Radio and television producers as well as comic-strip artists know this and have tried with some success to cash in on the implications of the mask.

In 1933, George Trendle, owner of station WXYZ in Detroit, called upon script-writer Fran Striker to invent the Lone Ranger, pasting him together from popular hero stereotypes in hopes of coming up with a children's radio show to compete with the big-network offerings. Trendle liked the idea of a Western, complete with masked bandit, but preferred a benevolent outlaw who, like Robin Hood, symbolized true justice and wholesome living. The masked rider that Striker created was indeed the personification of Good, at once a vigilante and an outlaw, a Texas Ranger and a bandit, destined to become a symbol of American freedom, self-reliance, adventure, and romance.

The Lone Ranger and his side-kick Tonto rode into overwhelming radio success. Before long they were featured in comic books, comic strips, novels, then finally on television. When the long-standing radio Lone Ranger, Earl W. Graser, a plump suburban lawyer whose cowboy experience was limited to a single ride on a grocer's delivery-cart horse, was killed in an automobile accident in 1941, the network contrived a way to preserve the dreams of so many young listeners. They explained away the newspaper obituaries by saying, Yes, everyone thinks he died, but he really is alive, seriously wounded, in hiding, and being nursed back to health by Tonto. When he recovers his strength he will have his revenge on the assailants who left him for dead. In the meantime, it serves his purposes to have the world believe he is dead. So, after a respectable interval of convalescence, the Lone Ranger was heard again, and most kids never realized his voice had changed. Brace Beemer was the Lone Ranger reincarnate.

This confusion of fact and fiction is the underlying method of the program. At one time, by contractual agreement, the actor who played the Lone Ranger was required either to appear masked as the Lone Ranger, or remain an anonymous, private citizen. He could not claim credit as an actor successfully portraying a character. The idea behind this arrangement was obviously to convince children that the Lone Ranger is real, someone they can believe in and not just another television or radio act.

Typical of this intermingling of truth and fiction is the anniversary show which used to appear annually on television to celebrate the origins of the Lone Ranger legend. The "history" vaguely echoes the network explanation of Graser's death. In addition, the anniversary story explained the mask. According to a CBS press release of January 8, 1957:

> " A patrol of six Texas Rangers in search of the notorious
> Butch Cavendish gang was ambushed by the outlaws and after the
> battle all the Rangers were left for dead.
> During the night, an Indian came upon the bodies by moonlight,
> discovered that one of the Rangers, though badly wounded,
> was still alive. The Indian carried him to a cave, where he
> bathed and dressed the wounds.
> For three days and nights he watched by the side of the
> unconscious Ranger. On the fourth day, the Ranger awoke
> and recognized the Indian as the same one who had saved his
> life years ago when both were boys.
> 'Your name is Tonto,' said the Ranger, 'and years ago you
> used to call me "Kemo Sabay." '
> 'You still "Kemo Sabay," ' replied Tonto. 'It means "Trusted
> Scout." You only Ranger left, you Lone Ranger.'

Then the Lone Ranger explained to Tonto that the outlaws knew him by sight and if they discovered he escaped death, they would track him down and do away with him. To make sure the Lone Ranger's identity would be concealed, Tonto prepared six graves and Kemo Sabay was 'buried' with his brother, who had commanded the Texas Rangers, and his friends.

Thereafter the Lone Ranger, to avoid being discovered by the Cavendish gang, hid his face behind a mask.   "

Because the mask supposedly hides the Ranger's true identity, it lends him a third dimension, that of reality. We know there is a real man behind the mask. Moreover, kids who saw the anniversary specials and knew who the Lone Ranger really was could enjoy a sense of participation in the conspiracy to keep the Lone Ranger alive.

Yet 55 per cent of the television audience for the show were adults. In a decade that longed for simple truths, for easy definitions of right and wrong, the Lone Ranger was Good. While McCarthy and cohorts found devils beneath the most innocent of masks, television audiences could switch the channel and find a man who was better than he appeared, a man whose mask protected his virtue.

As the personification of the fiction of the triumph of Good, the Lone Ranger drew accolades from high places. He was cited by Congressmen for furthering law and order in America. (Meanwhile, in the South also in mask, the KKK was riding, too, in pursuit of an illusive and subjective "law and order.")

Today a curious nostalgia for the 1950s centers around the television shows of that decade. Young people, who grew up under the influence of Howdy Doody, Hopalong Cassidy, and the Lone Ranger, can return to the security and simplicity of childhood through the medium of the rerun or the personal appearance. The Lone Ranger thus becomes their masquerade, their lost youth—what a hero would be if romance were only reality. Along with the rest of these old-timers, the masked rider has been taken out of mothballs to serve commercial interests. Clayton Moore, who today is bordering on the antique, still appears—sometimes without his costume, but always masked—in Aqua Velva and Glad Bag ads as well as local television reruns. The man may have gone to flab, but the mask is still taut and true, a symbol of professional devotion to American myth.

Comic strips and comic books are immediate reflections of popular culture. They are social satire without pretensions, revealing contemporary ideals and concerns, while claiming to be nothing more than entertainment.

It is significant, therefore, that many of the successful characters appearing in this medium have been masked: Batman, Captain Marvel, Captain America, Spider Man, the Lone Ranger, to name just a few. Others who do not wear masks may have disguises or alternate identities. The effectiveness of masks as dramatic devices, selling a particular character to the public, suggests that we have not outgrown Halloween.

In this century, Americans have been fascinated by the mask as a symbol of the alter ego, the other identity, the ability to move from role to role, to change one's physical appearance, to surmount the limitations of a particular situation. As society became more and more complex, the multiple identity became an obsession and an answer.

Victorian distinctions between the physical and the intellectual began the process of fragmentation. Industry completed the process, organizing lives into production lines. As more and more individuals moved from farming into industry, life grew less coherent: the family had nothing to do with the job; the job had nothing to do with the house; the house was not the place of business, and so on. Specialization also meant that scientists were at odds with humanists; sometimes the two schools of thought were at war within a single human body. Psychoanalysis was helping us to understand schizophrenia, while society continued to demand more and more complex role-playing. E.M. Forster cried out in warning, "Connect, only

connect. . . ."[69] Hermann Hesse seriously suggesting pasting the Magic Theatre together with humor.[70] The mask was another solution to the problem of fragmentation.

The film industry no doubt contributed to this solution. Film stars were being worshiped for the ability to wear the mask, for the duality of their existence on screen and off. Actors had always experienced this schizophrenia, but now it was obvious to the mass public. If movie stars could lead double and indeed triple lives, why shouldn't we all?

Organized crime also suggested the viability of an underground existence, an alternative society, operating within "legitimate" society and preying upon it.

And, finally, World War II convinced Americans that they could be Supermen, too, stepping dutifully out of the domestic environment to save the world with homemade strength and technology. We became a race of Sunday heroes.

Our comic books faithfully reflected this evolution. They featured men who could transform themselves from mere human beings into super beings; men who were reporters or writers from nine to five, scientific giants in their leisure time; men who with the flip of a mask could enter alien worlds; men who in disguise could solve the most complex of crimes, then like war heroes, return to the welcome trivia of home.

Even today, comic-book situations play upon the duality of life. The masks that comic-book characters wear represent their ability to negotiate these transformations with some degree of success. For example, Batman began his career in 1939, the surviving son of millionaire parents who were killed in a stick-up while walking home from a movie. Determined to prevent such tragedies from happening to other children, he devoted himself to physical fitness and science. Only when he completed this course of intensive body and mind building did he adopt the bat disguise and go out in pursuit of criminals, using his terrible aspect to strike terror into the hearts of superstitious lawbreakers.

141.

His batlike black mask seems relatively simple and unappalling in comparison to some of the models currently being featured in comic books. There are helmets, gas masks, diving gear, and armor, in addition to a variety of grotesque human faces. Occasionally, the mask has no real purpose other than being part of the uniform. Industry people do admit that the dramatic effect of the mask itself is enough to make a character popular.

If comic books are a social parody, reflecting in exaggerated form the veneer of our society, what they reflect is a world of masks. As for the readers of comic books, they are not innocent little children. The subject matter, based at least superficially on science and technology, would discourage tiny tots. The language of the comic book is consciously melodramatic, often quite sophisticated, incorporating word-plays and other literary devices. Again not for infants. And the advertisements are quite obviously geared to young people, young adults, dissatisfied with themselves and with their lives. There are muscle-building ads, weight-reducing ads, suggestions for attracting women, mail-order blanks for false mustaches. What all this suggests is that the comic book is itself a mask, the mode of escape from dissatisfaction and boredom into a world of excitement and adventure. It is a private, masked theatrical.

In earliest times, when the gods were behaving themselves, primitive witch doctors and members of secret societies would don their masks and cavort in order to entertain the villagers, especially the children.[71] Egyptian ceremonies involved acting out the roles of the gods in appropriate masks. Greek theatrical masks functioned as both sound equipment and scenery:

> " The stage masks of antiquity were of several kinds—namely, comic, tragic, and satiric—and they were called *personae*. The crudest and most vulgar of them, if not the oldest, were made of bark; others were leather, lined with cloth. They were sometimes constructed of light wood in order to insure the preservation of the model. The mask was proportioned to the

142.

size of the amphitheatre so that it could be seen clearly even from the farthest rows of seats. The carrying power of the voice was augmented by strips of brass fastened inside the mask near the mouth, or else the lips of the mask were widened and exaggerated in order to form a sort of rudimentary megaphone. Seen at close range, all of the masks, even the most comic, had a terrifying look about them, but if they had not been so crudely fashioned they would have seemed quite featureless at a distance.   "[72]

As the classical theater declined into Roman spectacles, masks were incorporated into the popular theater. Medieval mystery plays combined elements of the popular comic theater with religious morals, all *en masque*. Later masks were requisite for *commedia dell'arte* performances. Each role was a "mask" with its appropriate face covering, the inscrutable expression of these masks suggesting Oriental influences. By the middle of the sixteenth century, actors in this popular theater wore appropriate character masks while actresses, newly admitted to the stage, wore at least the black velvet *loup*.

At this time, too, the masque was evolving as a courtly form of drama, masked members of the Court alternating with professional actors in elaborate poetic interludes.

But as theater became increasingly concerned with middle class realities and verisimilitude replaced fantasy as the measure of theatrical success, cosmetics replaced masks as a means of achieving the desired effect.

*C*osmetics are the masks by which actors achieve realistic character portrayal. Stage make-up is not simply a thicker layer of street make-up. Intense lighting demands special cosmetics, and certain roles may call for an actor to age drastically or change appearance radically in the course of a single performance. This requires some serious mask-making.

The peculiarities of television and film broadcasting require an

143.

actor or performer to wear make-up in order to look natural. And because many people appear on television to sell themselves or something they represent, they want to look better than they usually do. A make-up artist skilled in the uses of optical illusion can "correct" some facial weaknesses using a variety of make-ups. For this reason, celebrities sometimes use one make-up artist for all television appearances: Ray Voege, a make-up artist with CBS, does Nixon's mask even when the President is appearing on other networks. Drastic transformations may require use of sculptural techniques and prosthetic devices. Science has provided the make-up man with a panoply of tools, many listed in Vincent Kehoe, Jr.'s book, *The Techniques of Film and Television Make-up:*

" absorbent cotton   foundation thinners   modeling tools
acetone   fluorescent make-up   *moulage*
adhesive tape   gauze   *mousseline de soie*
adhesives   gelatin capsules   mustache wax
alcohol   glycerin   nail polish
bandoline or hair-set gel hackle   nose putty
blood (artificial)   hair color spray   pencils
brilliantine   hair lacquer   powder
buckram   hair whitener   powder puffs
cheekcolor   lace or net   prosthetics
cleansing tissues   latex   razor blades
combs   lip gloss   rouge
crepe hair   lip colors   scar material
curling irons   lip-liner pencils   scissors
eye drops   make-up kit   sealers
eyelash curler   mascara   toupee tape
eyelashes   matte adhesive   vaseline
eye color   matte plasticized adhesive   waxes
foundations   metallic powders   wool crepe   "
                          mineral oil

144.

That's all it takes to create the theatrical mask of reality, to seem to be anyone at any time, even yourself.

Because of the nature of mass communication in the United States, politicians must be performers. The politician's theatrical mask is the carefully constructed public image that he wears. His image consists of his political views, his appearance, the people with whom he surrounds himself, his mode and style of speech, and his mannerisms as conveyed to the public through the various media. It is not the whole man, but rather the visible man.

> " A man displays an image by assuming a role in life. Selective aspects of his personality suitable to that role are emphasized and permitted public exposure; those not so suited are underplayed, compensated for by revealing 'other sides' of the man, or simply ignored. The image is not, therefore, that of the 'whole man,' but of dimensions of personality appropriate to the role and its setting. All the mass media may be used to portray candidates' images, but professional campaigners charged with the task of conveying positive pictures of their candidate—the image specialists—are particularly fond of newspapers, radio, and television for this purpose. "[73]

The politician's mask-makers are the men who conduct his political campaign, advise him, write his speeches, select his clothes, make him up for television and personal appearances. They are the image men.

Not a new breed by any means—only the latest generation of advertising men. Since the 1950s they have been making inroads on relatively "sacred" areas of modern life, from politics to corporate policy. The image men are remaking the world in their own image of what will sell. This is the logical extension of the American market ethic. At first it might seem an amusing hoax, but in the end it is serious business.

145.

A GROUP OF PEOPLE WEARING ENOCH POWELL FACSIMILE MASKS AND CLOTHES AT A CONSERVATIVE

PARTY CONFERENCE IN ENGLAND, 1970, SEEK THE POLITICIAN'S SUPPORT FOR SMALL TRADERS.

In 1969 J.B. Priestley published a satirical novel, *The Image Men*. Two scheming intellectuals set themselves up as image experts and formed first an educational institution and then a corporation, based on the absurd premise that they could manufacture and sell public images. They were glib and charming; and, much to their own surprise, their methods worked with telling effects on their clients' lives. Self-styled Professor Saltana advised:

" We are compelled to accept public images. First, because modern life is increasingly complex. We have to take more into account, especially in public life, than we can cope with, unless we are experts. Secondly, we are all strongly influenced by the mass media, which cannot do otherwise than simplify and so are inevitably concerned with images. You may dislike all this, Mrs. Lapford, just as I dislike seeing more and more motorcars and sometimes wish the internal-combustion engine had never been invented. But the cars are with us—and so are the images. We ignore them both at our peril. "[74]

How right he was. Today, largely because of television, politics consists of image-making. What matters is not the man behind the mask, but the mask itself—the way the man looks on television, the way he comes across in personal appearances, the way he conducts himself, his superficial style.

Only in the past decade or so has political image-making pretended to professional status. Even so, it is not governed by a formal organization; it is not based on a tested body of knowledge; there are no ethical standards by which to judge the work. Specialization per se and the impressive fee most political consultants collect qualify them as professionals. Yet the consultants themselves will insist upon their professional standing: One of them, Joseph Napolitan, says

" Politics is just hard work, so you use professionals. Today a candidate is more aware there are specialists in this business. It's like building a house. You can build it yourself. But the feasibility depends on the size of the house you want. You can hire experts, buy professional skills, get the best professional advice. It's like going to a doctor. There's nothing sinister involved. I advise candidates all the time. I'd be stupid not to learn something from my experience, something that can help someone else.   "

What the professional, political mask-makers seem to have learned is how best to combine the possibilities of the available technologies to sell their candidates. Occasionally, they can select a particularly attractive man; but more often they must take whoever can afford their considerable fees and then provide him with a viable mask.

The first step is to define the electorate, purchasers, or voters, and pinpoint the issues that concern them. This is where computer technology and modern polling techniques come into play. Already the simple opinion poll has been expanded into consumer-attitude surveys, designed to give the promoter a clear picture of what will and will not sell.

The next step is to present the candidate in such a way as to correspond with the indicated public needs. The outlines of the mask begin to fall into place. The candidate is briefed on what he is to say and how he is to say it, which issues to emphasize, which to play down. Occasionally, he is briefed on subjects he knows nothing about. At this point in the game, ethical problems arise. The image- or mask-makers are literally putting words into the candidate's mouth, teaching him what to think and say. According to Dan Nimmo, author of *The Political Persuaders*, "There are signs that in the dynamic relationship between the client-candidate and his manager, the tail wags the dog, and leaves a marked imprint on the political process in the wagging."[75] The mask-makers are making the masks the public buys: the masks, or politicians, do not make themselves.

Image-makers then choose the media that will work best for their candidate, to project his particular image and reach the electorate they have defined as potential buyers. Television undisputedly has the greatest impact; but it must be used carefully. Joseph Napolitan warns, "Every candidate must be very careful on television. You expose yourself on live TV, but you run the risk of getting killed crossing Fifth Avenue, too." Television is the medium of the mask, projecting a stance rather than an intelligence or even a personality. For this reason, Nixon's 1968 campaign advisers carefully reviewed tapes of his television appearances, analyzing the effect of words and mannerisms, taking notes to suggest to the candidate ways in which he might alter his style to take fuller advantage of the possibilities of the medium. In *The Selling of the President 1968*, Joe McGinniss insists that "the television celebrity is a vessel. An inoffensive container in which someone else's knowledge, insight, compassion, or wit can be presented. And we respond like the child on Christmas morning who ignored the gift to play with the wrapping paper." He goes on to say: "Television seems particularly useful to the politician who can be charming but lacks ideas."[76] Television is for masks.

Every President has his style, his characteristic phrases, his peculiar mannerisms, in short, his mask; but Nixon's seems particularly contrived, as if his mask-makers had made a puppet turned Frankenstein. The man acts as if he were wearing not only a mask, but also a full suit of armor.

> "He is the least 'authentic man' alive, the late mover, tester of responses, submissive to 'the discipline of consent.' A survivor. There is one Nixon only, though there seem to be new ones all the time—he will try to be what people want. He lacks the stamp of place or personality because the Market is death to style, and he is the Market's servant. His aim has always been the detached mind, calculating, freed for observing the free play of political idea, ready to go with the surviving one. This makes him stand for all that the kids find contrived, what they call 'plastic.' "[77]

There are characteristic Nixon gestures, some of which have

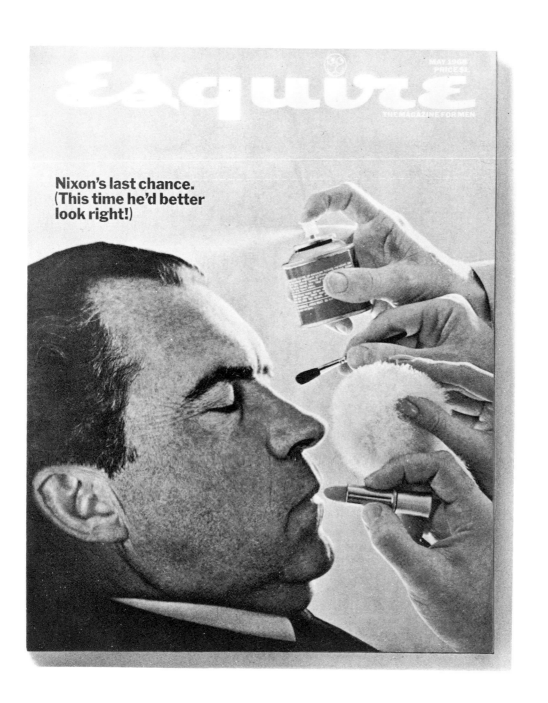

been eliminated from his repertory by his advisers, all of which reveal a physical awkwardness, a grinding of gears, There is a Nixon style of speech, a relentless simplification, punctuated by persistent and meaningless phrases, such as the now proverbial "Let me make one thing very clear," a peculiarly indirect way of coming at an issue by circumlocution, feeling his way around.

Clothes also contribute to the image. Nixon dresses formally, as if he were erecting one more barrier between himself and the world. Clothes are decorum; Nixon has survived all these years on restraint and decorum, on the negation of style. His is the mask of invisibility, of contrived formality, of facelessness. It has been suggested, perhaps not frivolously, that had he not been so ugly, he would have been a more honest politician—he would not have felt compelled to wear so elaborate a mask.

Still, according to one political consultant, "The public is not being conned—no more than when reading airline ads about how comfortable and great flying will be. We know better." Cynicism and experience will teach us to recognize the masks.

*T*o some extent, we, too, are masqueraders, trying to sell ourselves socially, in business, and in the privacy of our own minds. Each man sells an image, projecting his strengths, minimizing his weaknesses, presenting a viable face to the world, one which can be accepted, even acclaimed, as art. All the outward aspects of everyday life can contribute to this total image if used properly. Clothes, speech, gestures, and visible surroundings all contribute to the mask, which is the face that meets the world, the medium through which one confronts the unknown. The mask is in this broadest of interpretations a Jamesian setting, a social shell.

> "   By the shell I mean the whole envelope of circumstances. There's no such thing as an isolated man or woman; we're each of us made up of some cluster of appurtenances. What shall we call our 'self'? Where does it begin? Where does it

end? It overflows into everything that belongs to us—and then it flows back again. I know a large part of myself is in the clothes I choose to wear. I've a great respect for *things!* One's self for other people—is one's expression of one's self; and one's house, one's furniture, one's garments, the books one reads, the company one keeps—these things are all expressive. "[78]

We live within our masks. If they are well made, they will express the truth of individual being; if they are carelessly constructed, they become barriers. Masks are windows in a building, as transparent or murky as the circumstances of life demand. They can reveal the whole interior to the curious eye, they can open to accommodate some gesture of leaning. Or they can remain tightly closed, a seal against the world.

Reference Notes

1. R. Turner Wilcox, *Dictionary of Costume*. New York, 1969, page 385.
2. M. E. Hume-Griffith, *Behind the Veil in Persia and Turkish Arabia*. London, 1909, page 222.
3. J. Cordy Jefferson, *Historic Dress in America*, page 157.
4. Casey A. Wood, "The Wearing of Veils and Its Effect on Eyesight," 1896 (reprint of article).
5. Philip Stubbs, *The Anatomie of Abuses*. London, 1583.
6. Mary Evans, *Costume Throughout the Ages*. New York, 1950, page 139.
7. Mrs. Charles H. (E.J.) Ashdown, *British Costume during XIX Centuries*. New York, page 274.
8. Elsy Leuzinger, *The Art of Africa*. New York, 1967, pages 28, 29.
9. Francis Mossiker, *The Affair of the Poisons*. New York, 1969, page 149.
10. Molmenti's description is quoted in *Modesty in Dress* by James Laver, Boston, 1969.

11. Quoted in *Lights and Shadows of New York Life* by James D. McCabe, Jr., Facsimile Edition. New York, 1970, pages 604–611.

12. Ralph and Adelin Linton, *Halloween Through Twenty Centuries*. New York, 1950, page 8.

13. Charles Reich, *The Greening of America*. New York, 1971, page 237.

14. Charles Lerner, "History of Feminine Beautification," in *Archives of Dermatology and Syphilology*, vol. 26, December 1932, pages 1022–1031.

15. Dr. Henry Goodman, *Cosmetics and Your Skin*. New York, 1930, page 7.

16. C. H. Talbot, *Medicine in Medieval England*. London, 1967, page 146.

17. Geoffrey Chaucer, *The Romaunt of the Rose*, lines 1017–1020.

18. Jean Liébault, *Trois livres de l'embellissement et ornament du corps humain*. Paris, 1582, pages 24, 25.

19. William Shakespeare, *Hamlet*. Act III, scene i, line 150.

20. John Bulwer, *Anthropometamorphosis: Man Transformed; Or, the Artificial Changeling*. London, 1650, page 158.

21. William Salmon, *Polygraphice or the Arts of Drawing Limning Painting &c.* London, 1678 (first published in 1672), page 322.

22. *Ibid.*, page 326.

23. William Congreve, *The Way of the World*. Act IV.

24. "Cosmetics" in *The Encyclopaedia Britannica*. Chicago, 1971, vol. vi, page 565.

25. Mossiker, *op. cit.*

26. Richard Corson, *Stage Make-up*. New York, 1967, page 308.

27. Kellow Chesney, *The Anti-Society*. Boston, 1970, pages 239–41.

28. Thomas Hall, *The Queen's Royal Cookery . . . with several Cosmetick or Beautifying Waters*. London, 1710.

29. Quoted in *The Evolution of Plastic Surgery* by Maxwell Maltz. New York, 1946. page 30.

30. *Ibid.*, page 124.

31. *Ibid.*, pages 156, 157.

32. *Ibid.*, page 224.

33. Harriet La Barre, *Plastic Surgery: Beauty You Can Buy*. New York, 1970, page 50.

34. Joseph Needham, *Science and Civilisation in China*. Cambridge, 1971, vol. iv-1, pages 99ff.

35. "History of the Sun Glass," a Bausch & Lomb press release distributed by Ruder & Finn, Inc. New York, 1971.

36. Geoffrey Chaucer, *The Wife of Bath's Tale*, lines 1203–1204.

37. William Shakespeare, *King Lear*, Act IV, scene vi, line 175

38. William Shakespeare, *As You Like It*. Act II, scene vii, line 156.

39. James R. Gregg, *The Story of Optometry*. New York, 1965, page 55.

40. "History of the Sun Glass," *op. cit.*, page 2.

41. Saint Jerome, Letter 54 in *Familiar Quotations*. John Bartlett. Boston, 1968, page 145.

42. John Hunter, *A Manual for Bee-Keeping*. London, 1875, page 175.

43. Leuzinger, *op. cit.*, page 29.

44. Alfred Hutton, *Old Sword-Play*. London, 1892, page 2.

45. Quoted in *Baseball—The Early Years* by Harold Seymour. New York, 1960, page 64.

46. Dean Hill, *Football Through the Years*. New York, 1940, page 73.

47. Paul Wirz, *Exorcism and the Art of Healing in Ceylon*. Leiden, 1954, pages 25, 26.

48. Terence McLaughlin, *Dirt*. New York, 1971, page 25.

49. Elie Benveniste, "*Recherches Expérimentales sur l'action protectrice du Masque dans les maladies infectieuses*." Thèse présenté à la Faculté de Médecine de l'Université de Lausanne, 1919, page 2.

50. *San Francisco Chronicle*, October 25, 1918.

51. Robert H. Davis, *Breathing in Irrespirable Atmospheres*. London, 1947, page 165.

52. *Ibid.*, page 166.

53. *Ibid.*, page 287.

54. Sir Robert Henry Davis, *Deep Diving and Submarine Operations*. London, 1951.

55. This is a blank in the manuscript of Dr. Richard Pococke's book, *Travels in England*. London, 1754.

56. Quoted in *Deep Diving and Submarine Operations, op. cit.*, page 557.

57. Davis, *op. cit.*, page 573.

58. Tighe Hopkins, *The Man in the Iron Mask*. New York, 1901.

59. Allen W. Trelease, *White Terror*. New York, 1971, page xi.

60. *Ibid.*, page 56.

61. John Lawrence, *A History of Capital Punishment*. New York, 1960, pages 41, 42.

62. Quoted in Lawrence, *op. cit.*, page 89.

63. Christopher Hibbert, *Highwaymen*, New York, 1967, page 55.

64. From a poem by Andrew Marvell, written August 9, 1671, quoted in the essay "Colonel Thomas Blood, Crown-Stealer," by Professor W. Abbott, included in the book, *Pirates, Highwaymen and Adventurers*, edited by Eric Partridge. London, 1927, page 81.

65. Wilbur Cortz Abbott, *Conflicts with Oblivion*. New Haven, 1924, page 152.

66. Francis Jackson, *Jackson's Recantation, Or, The Life & Death of the Notorious High-way-man, now Hanging in Chains at Hampstead*. London, 1674.

67. Hibbert, *op. cit.*, pages 34, 35.

68. Joseph Henry Jackson, *Bad Company*. New York, 1949, pages 130, 131.

69. E. M. Forster, *Howard's End*. New York, 1921, pages 186–87.

70. Hermann Hesse, *Steppenwolf*. New York, 1963.

71. Leuzinger, *op. cit.*, page 29.

72. Pierre Louis Duchartre, *The Italian Comedy*. New York, 1966, page 44.

73. Dan Nimmo, *The Political Persuaders*. Englewood Cliffs, New Jersey, 1970, page 129.

74. J. B. Priestley, *The Image Men*. Boston, 1969, page 25.

75. Nimmo, *op. cit.*, page 67.

76. Joe McGinniss, *The Selling of the President, 1968.* New York, 1969, page 22.

77. Gary Wills, "Richard Nixon, The Last Liberal," in *The Washington Monthly,* October 1970, page 25.

78. Henry James, *The Portrait of a Lady.* Boston, 1956, pages 172–73.

Illustration Sources

Bettmann Archive: 37, 55, 68, 71, 86, 91, 99, 102, 112, 125
Cambridge University Library: 80
Culver Pictures, Inc.: 137, 155
Carl Fischer, Esquire Magazine: 151
Henry Grossman, Life Magazine © Time Inc.: 17
Hiro, Harper's Bazaar: 65
NASA: 106, 107
Sport & General: 146, 147
Pete Turner: 24, 25
UPI: 5, 8, 9, 11, 43, 47, 49, 52, 57, 59, 61, 63, 66, 67, 76, 82, 85, 89, 94, 97, 103, 121, 127, 133, 134
Henry Wolf: 39

*T*his book has been designed by Samuel N. Antupit, who is grateful to Sarina Bromberg for her assistance and patience.

The text has been set in types designed by Giambattista Bodoni of Parma in the late eighteenth century. The title and chapter openings have been set in Thorowgood Italic, designed in England by Robert Thorne in the late nineteenth century. The book has been printed by Halliday Lithographing Company on alpine vellum opaque and bound by Montauk Book in cloth from Columbia Mills.